THE LIFE OF THE I

by

FATHER LOUIS COULANGE

Translated from the French by
STEPHEN HADEN GUEST

1930
NEW YORK
ALFRED A. KNOPF

SET IN MONOTYPE FOURNIER
AND PRINTED IN GREAT BRITAIN
FOR ALFRED A. KNOPF INC.
BY THE EDINBURGH PRESS
EDINBURGH

Kessinger Publishing's Rare Reprints
Thousands of Scarce and Hard-to-Find Books!

- •
- •
- •
- •
- •
- •
- •
- •
- •
- •
- •
- •
- •
- •
- •
- •
- •
- •
- •
- •
- •

We kindly invite you to view our extensive catalog list at:
http://www.kessinger.net

SATAN THROWN OUT OF HEAVEN

By an unknown painter of the fifteenth century, in the
Musée Calvet at Avignon

PREFACE

THE author is a French priest and theologian who has adopted a pseudonym because of the unorthodox nature of his speculations. He traces the emergence of the personality of Satan, the Evil One, from the epoch of the monotheistic religion of the Jews—when only an impersonal "evil inclination" was recognised—through the progressively substantial revelations of the New Testament, the Early Fathers, and the Mediæval Theologians, to the culmination of fleshly-phantasmal horror in the fifteenth and sixteenth centuries, when the fears and desires of a populace that was beginning to get free from feudal repressions triumphed—in so many directions—over the traditional wisdom of the Church.

When national governments had managed to obtain sufficient authority, witchcraft and devilry of all kinds were first transferred from the Church's jurisdiction to their own : then regarded as matters of fraud or of natural rather than of supernatural affliction.

With steadily increasing disbelief in his reality, the Devil shrinks to a mere shadow of his Renascence self (for it is the Renascence, not the Middle Ages, which developed the most vivid preoccupation with devilry), but Father " Coulange " ends his book not with conventional optimism, but by showing that the underlying enigma of evil, the conflict between belief in an Omnipotent Good God, and perceptions of pain and futility, remains as obscure as ever ; though modern men, and their priests of all denominations,

v

repress, with the aid of the narcotics of " social solidarity "
and " the progress of science," any fundamental consideration of it.

Father Coulange's book is an opportune corrective of the
contemporary revival of half-belief in all manner of Black
Magic, Spirit-manœuvring, and Devil Worship.   His
learning is as extensive as his logic is acute, and, following,
essentially, in the footsteps of the great masters of doctrine,
he disentangles man's externalised projections of his desires
from the fundamental mysteries of the universe.

Incidentally, the " ordinary general reader " will obtain
many very interesting glimpses into the thought and feeling
of some of the greatest men of the Christian past, for a third
of the book consists of illustrative quotation from such as
Lactantius, Irenæus, Origen (whose view of the creation of
the material universe is curiously like the hypotheses of
certain modern physicists) : Ambrose, Jerome, Augustine :
Bede, Duns Scotus, Albertus Magnus : Aquinas, Suarez,
Luther.

CONTENTS

PART THREE

THE ACTIVITIES OF THE DEVIL ON EARTH BEFORE THE FOUNDATION OF THE CHURCH

PART FOUR

ACTIVITIES OF THE DEVIL SINCE THE FOUNDATION OF THE CHURCH

LIST OF ILLUSTRATIONS

xi

A TRANSLATION OF THE PACT OF
URBAIN GRANDIER (p. 176).

Monseigneur et Maistre. I acknowledge you as my God, I promise to serve you for the rest of my life, and from now on, I renounce all other Gods, Jesus Christ, the Virgin Mary, all the Saints of Heaven, the Roman Catholic and Apostolic Church, and all the prayers and supplications which it may make on my behalf. I promise to worship you, to do you homage at least three times each day, and to teach evil to as many persons as I may. Willingly I renounce Baptism and all the goodness of Jesus Christ, and lest I should wish to be converted, I now give you my body, my soul and my life, holding these from you, I having dedicated them to you for ever without any wish for repentance.

Signed   *URBAIN GRANDIER*
with his blood.

INTRODUCTION

OVER against God, who loves mankind and is pleased to load men with His benefits, Christian dogma places a being who aspires only to do evil, to harm mankind; a being who is, in a manner, God's obverse.

This evil-doing personage has beneath his dominion an innumerable army of satellites, who carry out his orders and are called demons. He himself is sometimes called Satan, sometimes the Prince of This World, the Evil One, Lucifer. But his principal name is, the Devil.

We propose to relate here the history of the Devil and of his evil activities. He will be considered first as to his own nature: his origin, his wiles, the conditions of his existence will be described. Then the warfare he wages against mankind will be related, and that also which the Church is forced to carry on against him to defend her children. Since the captain is inseparable from his subordinates, one cannot speak of the Devil without mentioning the demons who obey his orders: and the origin of their subjection will be investigated. In the course of our research throughout Antiquity and the Middle Ages, our guides will be, firstly, Holy Writ, and secondly, the Fathers, escorted by the great Theologians. And if the reader observe that the Devil has not escaped from the great law of evolution, the proof of this will have been furnished him by the authorised interpreters of the thought of the Church.

It is thus, above all, a chapter of the history of theology which is here set forth. Faithful to his rôle of chronicler, the author will content himself with citing the texts, and will leave to each reader the task of comprehending them. Nevertheless, after receiving the depositions of the Fathers and the Theologians, he cannot omit to consult, as well, science and general history, which declare themselves in possession of important information. He will note their testimony too. And thus, here and there, this enquiry will cross the boundaries of theology, within which it will, as a rule, remain confined.

PART ONE

THE ORIGIN AND FALL OF THE DEVIL

The Devil of the Christian Church is an evil being.
But he has not always been such. His perversity is his
own personal fault. He was good in the beginning,
and it was a sin which made him what he is now.
What rank did he occupy in the hierarchy of beings
before his downfall? And what was the sin which
wrought his undoing?

Λ

CHAPTER I

THE ORIGINAL STATE OF THE DEVIL

THE Fathers, who were above all preoccupied with describing the wickednesses committed by the Devil when he had become guilty, did not, usually, go further. They did not think of enlightening us as to the state of this personage before his fall. Those amongst them whose attention was attracted to this side of the subject have said, or indicated, that Satan was, in the beginning, the first of the angelic spirits. Tertullian (*Adversus Marcionem*, 2, 10)[1] writes of him:

' He was born the wisest of all the angels, before being the Devil: I am not aware that wisdom is an evil. Read through the prophecy of Ezekiel 28 12; thou wilt see clearly that he was born good and that he became evil by his will. The following words are addressed to the Devil under the symbolic name of the King of Tyre: " Son of man, take up a lamentation for the king of Tyre, and say unto him, Thus saith the Lord God: Thou sealest up the sum (which means, Thou art the integral expression of image and of resemblance);

[1] The names of the Fathers and Theologians, and of their works, have been given in the forms most commonly adopted by the leading English theologians : that is to say, sometimes in Latin, sometimes in English.—*Translator.*

3

full of wisdom and perfect in beauty (because he was the most eminent of the angels, the chief of the angels, the wisest of all); thou wast in Eden the garden of God . . . thou wast the anointed cherub that covereth; and I set thee, so that thou wast upon the holy mountain of God; thou hast walked up and down in the midst of the stones of fire. Thou wast perfect in thy ways from the day that thou wast created, till unrighteousness was found in thee. . . ." '

Many are the Fathers who, following Tertullian, thought to discern the Devil in the king of Tyre of Ezekiel's prophecy, and these, similarly, considered Satan the first of all the angels.

Lactantius expresses the same thought in a strange text, which it is important to place before the reader (*Divinæ Institutiones*, 2, 9):

' God, before creating the world, produced a spirit similar to himself and filled with the virtues of God the Father. He then made another in whom the imprint of the divine origin did not remain. For he was tainted with the venom of jealousy and thus passed from good to evil. . . . He was jealous of his elder brother who, remaining attached to God the Father, obtained his affection. This being who, from good which he was, became evil, is called Devil by the Greeks.'

Thus, according to Lactantius, the Devil is a younger brother of the Word; but a brother who developed evilly, while his elder, by his goodwill, deserved his Father's affection.

Gregory of Nyssa, in his *Catechetical Lectures*, 6, 5, tells us, in order to show us that the Devil was, in the beginning, the first of the angels, that God confided to him the government of the earth. Saint Gregory the Great, having to explain the text of Job xl. 14, where the crocodile is spoken of under the name of Behemoth, shows easily that the crocodile is a symbol for the Devil, and he says (*Morals*, 32, 47):

'Behemoth is called the chief of the ways of God because God began in him the work of creation and placed him above the other angels.'

In his *Homilies upon the Gospels*, 34, 7, we read:

'The following prophecy of Ezekiel 28, 12,[1] refers to the angel who was created first: Thou sealest up the sum, full of wisdom and perfect in beauty; thou wast in Eden, the garden of God. . . . This angel was above all the angelic orders who, by contrast, increased yet more his glory.'

But, at this period, the pretender who passed himself off as the Areopagite, the disciple of Saint Paul, came to revolutionise the world of the angels, and to decide, among other innovations, that the spirits of the superior orders had no contact with the earth. This assertion had an unforeseen consequence. Saint John of Damascus (*De fide orthodoxe*, 2, 3 and 4), reading in Gregory of Nyssa that Satan was, in the beginning, charged with the government of the world and, in the *Areopagite*, that the superior angels

---

[1] The Revised Version has been used for texts from the Bible.— *Translator*.

had no contact with the world, reconciles these two authorities by relegating the Devil to the lower ranks of the angelic world. Thus he turned against the traditional interpretation the text of Saint Gregory of Nyssa, which was meant to support it. The traditional interpretation was defended, and the Devil occupied the first place. But there still remained something of the Damascene's assertion. Out of regard for this doctor, no one dared to attack as heresy the opinion of which he was the defender. And the supremacy of the Devil was given as a probable opinion with which one has the right to disagree without incurring any censure. Saint Thomas says, in the *Summa*, 1, 63, 7 :

> ' Gregory says that the angel who sinned was superior to all. And that seems the more probable.'

And we read in Suarez, *De Angelis*, 7, 16, 8 :

> ' It appears more probable that Lucifer belonged to the first hierarchy, that in this hierarchy he belonged to the first order, that he was among the first of this order.'

In reality, while they avoided affirmation, they had no doubt. They believed that Satan had occupied the first rank among the celestial spirits. And as, since the reform of the *Areopagite*, the first order of the angelic world was constituted by the seraphim, the Devil was no longer the ' cherub that was upon the holy mountain of God ' of whom the prophecy of Ezekiel speaks ; he was held to be a seraph. And the only doubtful point was to know whether, before his fall, he was superior to all the seraphim, or whether he had equals; if he was the most perfect creature, or if he was only one of the members of the most perfect order. Opinions were divided. Some, with Saint Thomas,[1] placed the Devil above all creatures, others thought that he had had equals and that Saint Michael, notably, was not inferior to him.[2]

[1] Saint Thomas was led to this result by his theory of the principle of individuation (see Perrin, *Somme theologique*, 1, 35, 37).

[2] *Suarez*, 7, 16, 11.

CHAPTER II

THE FALL OF THE DEVIL

WE read in *Genesis* vi. 2 :

'The sons of God beheld the daughters of men, that they were fair; and they took them wives of all that they chose.'

Who were these 'sons of God?' The *Book of Enoch* answers this question in the following passage (vi. 1) which, evidently, is intended as a paraphrase of the text of *Genesis:*

'When the children of men had multiplied, in those days were born unto them beautiful and comely daughters. And the angels, the children of heaven, saw and lusted after them and said to one another: "Come, let us choose us wives from among the children of men and beget us children."'

Thus, according to the *Book of Enoch*, the 'sons of God' of whom *Genesis* speaks were angels. This interpretation found acceptance among the first Fathers, beginning with Saint Justin, who says (2 *Apologia*, 5, 2) :

'God confided the care of men and of things terrestrial to angels. But the angels, violating this order, had commerce with the women and had by them children who are the demons.'

§ 1. IT IS ATTRIBUTED FIRST TO JEALOUSY

But one would err if one sought here the origin of the fall of the Devil. According to the first Fathers, the fall of the Devil had nothing in common with the fall of the evil angels. It had its origin, not in concupiscence, but in jealousy of Adam.

The theory of jealousy is sketched out by Justin, who explains that the Devil became evil when he induced Eve to sin; he authorises us to deduce, as a consequence, that, before deceiving our first mother, Satan was not yet evil; but he does not tell us the motive of Satan's conduct. This is his text (*Dialogue*, 124, 3):

'There was a fall of one of the chiefs; he who was called the serpent fell with a profound fall, for having led Eve astray.'[1]

With Irenæus, the doctrine is set forth in the full light of day. We learn when and how the angel to-day called Devil became evil:

'4, 40, 3: The angel became apostate and an enemy on the day when he became jealous of God's creature and undertook to set him against God.'

'5, 24, 4: The Devil who, according to S. Paul's teaching in the Epistle to the Ephesians 2, 2, was one of the angels meant for the air, became apostate and a rebel from the Divine law when he became jealous of man; for jealousy drives one from God.'

[1] Athenagoras, too, is far from precise. He says (*Legatio*, 24) that Satan, set by God at the head of the government of the world, proved negligent and evil-disposed in the exercise of his functions.

Tertullian, after teaching that the Devil came forth pure from the hands of God, and that he himself perverted himself, tells us when this perversion took place (*Adversus Marcionem*, 2, 10):

'What offences, then, are imputed to him? He has turned man aside from the submission he owed to God. He has sinned ever since he sowed sin.'

And the following text teaches us that the motive of the Devil, when he urged man to sin, was jealousy (incorrectly called impatience), *De patientia*, 5:

'I observe that impatience is born of the Devil, who gave himself up to impatience when he saw that the Lord had subjected to his image, that is to say, to man, all created beings. For if he had endured this state of things, he would not have felt any pain; and if he had not felt any pain, he would not have been jealous of man. So true is it that he deceived man because he was jealous . . . knowing from his own experience how efficacious for leading one into sin impatience was, that impatience which he was the first to know and *through which he had entered into sin.* It was to impatience that he had recourse in order to make man sin.'

Thus, according to Tertullian, the Devil was good until the day when he was jealous of Adam's destiny, and it was jealousy that was his first sin. Such also is the opinion of Saint Cyprian, as is proved by this passage from his book, *Concerning jealousy and envy*:

'See whence cometh jealousy, see when and how it made its first appearance. . . . It is to jealousy that, from the beginning of the world, the Devil owes his ruin, and also that he has been a cause of ruin. This angel, who was majestic and cherished by God, was precipitated into jealousy when he saw man created in God's image. And jealousy made him fall himself before leading him to work the fall of man.'

We find the doctrine of jealousy again at the beginning of the fourth century, in Lactantius. But it is profoundly modified. We know that, according to this doctor, God engendered, before the creation of the world, two sons—the Word and the Devil. The latter, who was younger than the Word, was jealous of his elder brother. This jealousy made him a liar, while the Word deserved, by his perseverance, the affection of his Father.

We return to the tradition of Justin and of Irenæus with Gregory of Nyssa, who writes as follows (*Catechetical Lectures*, 6, 5):

' The supreme authority assigned to each of the angelic powers his duty in the administration of the universe. To one of these powers was confided the government of the earth. Next there was formed a terrestrial creature which was the image of the power on high. This living creature is— man. In him there dwelt the divine beauty of intelligent nature mingled with a secret force. The being charged with the government of the earth thought himself offended and humiliated when, from nature, subjected to his orders, he saw come forth a substance made in the image of the sovereign dignity.'

§ 2. THE FALL OF THE DEVIL IS NEXT ATTRIBUTED TO PRIDE

But in this Gregory of Nyssa was a belated conservative. By his time jealousy had given place to pride; the Devil, who had begun by being jealous of man, had become proud and in rebellion against God. The author of this transformation was the great Alexandrian doctor, Origen.

It was neither chance nor caprice which led Origen to this conclusion. He was brought to it by the exigencies of his metaphysics. According to him, the angelic spirits were alone existent in the original plan of creation, and they alone ought to have existed. The material world was only drawn forth from the void on the day when the angels became guilty, and its purpose was to serve as a prison for the erring spirits. According to this principle, the Devil, like the other perverse angels, had already fallen into sin when the material world began to exist. Definitely, therefore, his fall was previous to the creation of Adam. Jealousy of man could not explain it. It was necessary to seek something different: Origen sought it.

In chapter xiv of *Isaiah*, there is a passage of sheer poetry, where we see the king of Babylon, who has just died, descend into hell. On learning of the arrival of this proud potentate, the souls of the dead kings rise up and, as soon as he appears, present to him their ironic homage in the following terms:

' Art thou also become weak as we ? Art thou

become like unto us ? Thy pomp is brought down to hell. . . . How art thou fallen from heaven, O day star, son of the morning! how art thou cut down to the ground, which didst lay low the nations! And thou saidst in thine heart, I will ascend into heaven, I will exalt my throne above the stars of God; and I will sit upon the mount of congregation, in the uttermost parts of the north : I will ascend above the heights of the clouds ; I will be like unto the Most High.'

This speech struck Origen profoundly. He observed several traits which, according to him, could not apply to an earthly king and were suitable only to a celestial spirit. There was no doubt that the fall of the Devil was meant, the fall of him who, in Saint John, is called the prince of this world, and whom Saint Paul names as the prince of the powers of the air. Origen concludes (*De Principiis*, 1, 5, 5 ; 4, 22 ; *Homilies upon Numbers*, 12, 4) that Satan was originally an angelic spirit who was led into sin through pride.

Origen's interpretation was accorded a sympathetic reception ; the fourteenth chapter of *Isaiah* became a classic reference, and Satan became the prince of pride, on whose brow was to be read :

'I will be like unto the Most High.'

Naturally, the Greek Church was the first to follow the way traced out by its great doctor. In it, it early became habitual to interpret the fall of Satan by *Isaiah*, and to explain that the Devil, before tempting man, had already sinned through pride. This is what Eusebius writes (*Præparatio Evangelica*, 7, 16) :

' He who, after being the first to fall, made others fall . . . is usually called Dragon, Serpent. . . . The divine books explain in these terms the cause of his fall. . . . How art thou fallen from heaven, O Lucifer, son of the morning! . . . thou saidst in thine heart, I will ascend unto heaven . . . I will be like unto the Most High. This teaches us that, in the beginning jewelled with the divine virtues, he fell through his pride and through his revolt against God.'

In the West, Saint Hilary, Saint Ambrose and Saint Jerome familiarised themselves with the writings of Origen. It was through them that the theory of pride penetrated into the Latin Church.

Hilary, commentating a text of *Isaiah*, where an individual gives himself up to boasting, says (*In Ps.*, 118, 16, 7) :

' This speech is that of the proud, that is to say, of the Devil, who dared to say to our God and Lord Jesus Christ, when he showed him the kingdoms of the earth in all their glory : All these things will I give thee, if thou wilt fall down and worship me.'

In another place, commentating a text where there is mention of mountains, he says (*In Ps.*, 64, 8) :

' These mountains indicate all the eminent powers that rise up and revolt against God and thus incur his anger. God the Word came down to earth after taking on a human nature and first lowered the summits of these mountains ; I mean that he broke the rebellious dignity of the Devil and of his hosts.'

Saint Ambrose is more precise than Saint Hilary. He says (*In Ps.*, 118, 7, 8) :

' It was through pride that the Devil himself fell from grace. For it was on the day when he cried : " I will exalt my throne above the stars of God . . . I will be like unto the Most High . . .," that he was cast forth from the company of the angels.'

And elsewhere (*In Ps.*, 118, 16, 15) :

' How should he not treat with pride God's servants, he who rises up against God, saying : " I will ascend into heaven . . . I will ascend above the heights of the clouds . . . I will be like unto the Most High ? " How should he conform to truth in his relations with men, he who makes boast to be the equal of the Lord ? '

Saint Jerome, writing to Eustochium, daughter of Paula, says to her (*Ep.*, 22, 27) :

' I know that neither you nor your mother are tainted by the pride which made the Devil fall.'

In his letter to Oceanus he says that the episcopal dignity makes those who receive it without first passing through lower functions proud. And he adds (*Ep.*, 69, 9) :

' Now it is certain that the Devil was lost through his arrogance.'

In his *Commentary upon Psalm* cxix. 2, speaking of the sins of the tongue, he says (*Anecdota Maredsoliana*, 3, 2, 224) :

'How did the Devil fall ? Was it after a theft, a murder, an adultery? In truth, these things are sins, but it was not for that, that the Devil fell. He fell because of his tongue. What did he say ? He said : "I will ascend into heaven. . . I will exalt my throne above the stars of God . . . I will be like unto the Most High." '

Saint Augustine made himself the disciple of the three above-mentioned doctors. In his *Homilies upon the Psalms* we read (*In Ps.*, 58, 2, 5) :

'It is solely because of pride that the Devil will be punished. He is verily the first of all sinners. . . . He did not become guilty of adultery nor of drunkenness, nor of fornication, nor of theft ; it was pride alone that made him fall.'

Augustine was scarcely to be contradicted, and thus the Latin Church completely forgot the doctrine that Saint Irenæus, Tertullian and Saint Cyprian had taught.

THE FALL OF THE REBEL ANGELS

A fresco by Spinello Aretino in the Church of St Angelo at Arezzo

CHAPTER III

IN WHAT HAS THE PRIDE OF THE DEVIL CONSISTED?

SINCE the fourth century, the Devil had fallen through pride. What was the objective of his pride? An insoluble problem, if we are to judge by the multiple solutions that the doctors have presented, none of which has succeeded in establishing itself.

Let us first see the state of affairs before Suarez:

§ I. BEFORE SUAREZ

Saint Augustine, whose opinion would have become law, scarcely touched the question. When the problem of the pride of the Devil arose in his path, he eluded it by a few summary formulæ, whence no precise thought can be disentangled. Augustine believes, because of the text of *Isaiah*, that Satan wished to be 'like unto God'; but he never asked himself how that had come about.

Some time before Augustine, Saint Gregory of Nazianzus says (*Lectures*, 35, 5) that the Devil wished to pass himself off as God. Prudentius explained (*Hamartigenia*, 168) that the Devil sought to make his companions believe that he had himself created himself, and that he had created matter out of his own body. Then came Saint Gregory the Great (*Morals*, 34, 40), who reproached Satan with having wished to be his own master and with having sought to shatter the bonds of dependence which attach him to God.

Saint Anselm invoked the aid of argument to solve the problem of the pride of the Devil. According to him (*De casu diaboli*, 4) Satan did not desire to be God ; but he wished to obtain beatitude before the time fixed by his creator. Thus he opposed his will to that of his sovereign master. He behaved himself in some sort as a God ; therein lay his fault. A little after Anselm, Rupert (*De Victoria Verbi Dei*, 1, 8-12) took up once more the theory of Prudentius ; if one were to believe him, Satan wished to make himself adored as a God by the other angels. A number among them let themselves be duped ; they believed that Satan had not been drawn forth from the void, and that he had within himself the source of his existence.

Anselm's theory attracted the attention of Albertus Magnus, who adopted it (in *Sententias*, 2, 5, 3). Saint Thomas, also, took it for himself, not, however, without perfecting it. First of all, he demolished the other opinions (*Summa*, 1, 63, 3). He showed that Satan could not have been so extravagant as to wish to be God, or independent of God. Having thus cleared the ground, he made use of Anselm's views. But Anselm had treated of beatitude without pre-occupation with the distinctions between the natural and the supernatural order. Saint Thomas was more precise. He taught that the sin of Satan had consisted either in rejecting supernatural happiness and contenting himself with happiness in agreement with the exigencies of his own nature, or else in thinking to obtain supernatural happiness through his own powers and without the help of grace. He observed that, in either hypothesis, Satan had wished to derive his happiness from himself alone, and thus he had, in a certain sense, sought to make himself like unto God.

Here and there in the writings of the Fathers there are expressions according to whose terms Satan wished to be God. But no one took these formulæ literally, and none of the doctors whom we have hitherto examined believed that the pride of the Devil consisted in wishing to possess the divine nature. In the fourteenth century Duns Scotus made himself the apostle of this opinion, which, heretofore, no one had upheld.[1] He thought he could demonstrate that there had been too much haste in declaring the desire for divinity impossible. Doubtless the Devil had not been able to imagine himself as being capable of becoming God, nor, consequently, of working to become him. But besides the absolute and efficacious desire which strives towards a possible end, there is the conditional desire which wishes that such an end were possible. Now the Devil could have felt a desire of this nature ; he could have regretted that divinity was a good beyond his reach. After developing this consideration, Duns Scotus

[1] In *Sententias*, 2, 5, 1.

takes the text of *Isaiah :* ' I will be like unto the Most High,' and he concludes that Satan had indeed desired divinity in the aforesaid manner.

§ 2.   SUAREZ

There was no lack of explanations to account for the pride of Satan. It remained to discover what these explanations were worth. Suarez submitted them one after another to a judicious and impartial criticism.[1] First he considered the theory of an inordinate desire for beatitude, and he showed its vanity.

' If the Devil,' he says, ' wished to retain natural beatitude without desiring to raise himself to the supernatural beatitude that God offered him, however one may explain his refusal, one cannot make him sin through pride. The personage drunk with his natural happiness to the point of refusing another superior to it is not he of whom Isaiah speaks, who seeks to raise himself above his condition : he does not correspond to the definition given by Scripture. And if it is said that Satan did not reject supernatural happiness, but desired to obtain it by his own powers and without the aid of grace, we shall scarcely be more advanced. How could Satan have believed that he was capable of attaining supernatural happiness by himself ? A supernatural good is, by its very definition, a good that surpasses nature. How then could the prince of the angels not have seen that there was a contradiction in seeking to do a thing which sur-

[1] *De angelis,* 7, 10–14.

passed his nature ? To rise into the air without wings
is an insanity which no reasonable man thinks of. Is
it not objectionable to attribute to an angelic spirit
a theory of which a reasonable man is incapable ?
However, let us admit that some such aberration had
entered into the spirit of the Devil. We can thus
make him commit a sin of heresy, but not a sin of
pride. We obtain a precursor of Pelagius ; but
Pelagius did not say " I will be like unto the Most
High." '

After reducing Saint Thomas' theory to fragments,
Suarez passes to that of Duns Scotus and inflicts the
same fate upon it. Duns Scotus, as we have seen,
dared not lend the Devil the intention of becoming
God ; he attributed to him only a velleity in that
direction. Suarez replied that, taken literally, such a
velleity could not constitute a sin. It would have to
be considered as one of those extravagant thoughts
which cross the minds of all of us, without making
us guilty, because we do not dwell on them and
because we cannot dwell on them. If Duns Scotus
went further and lent to Satan a positive regret that
he could not be God, without doubt he made him
a great sinner, but he could not obtain this result
save at the price of a chimerical hypothesis, inasmuch
as this alleged regret would offend the intellect of
a celestial spirit. And finally if, granting the impossible, Satan had felt regret at not being God, at least
he was unable to work to become God. From then
on, the picture of the Devil drawn by Duns Scotus
did not correspond with the Scriptural model. His
Satan did not say, like him of *Isaiah :* ' I will ascend

above the heights of the clouds ; I will be like unto the Most High.' The latter hoped to achieve his desires ; such was not the case with the erring being imagined by Duns Scotus.

Suarez was equally merciless to the ancient theory according to which the Devil had wished to make himself independent of God. He replied that such a pretension supposed, like the desire to be equal to God, an aberration of which an angel was incapable. Satan could not forget that he was a creature, and that he was, because of this, infinitely beneath God, his creator. When it was found impossible to reproach the Devil with an inordinate love of independence, he was accused of having sought to dominate the other angels. Others added this second crime to the first, and made Satan factious and ambitious at the same time. But, replied Suarez, one can only desire that which one has not. Satan, being the most perfect creature that came forth from the hands of God, surpassed all the angels by the gifts of nature ; he surpassed them all equally by the gifts of grace proportionate to the gifts of nature. This superiority gave him the right to command them. He could not, therefore, desire anything that he had not already : and the hypothesis of ambition explains his sin no better than the hypothesis of independence.

It was not sufficient to demolish : it was still necessary to construct : and, having overthrown all the hypotheses by which the sin of the Devil had until then been explained, it was necessary to find a new one. Suarez had one to his hand.

At about the time of the Council of Trent, certain

theologians put forward the idea that God had, from the beginning, made known to the angels his project of hypostatically uniting the Word and human nature, and that Satan had been offended at seeing the privilege of hypostatic union accorded to a member of the human race instead of to the most perfect creature, that is to say, to himself.[1] Suarez was seduced by this theory. All the other explanations either supposed that Satan had lost common sense to an extraordinary degree, or else made him commit a sin in which pride had no part, or even imputed to him as a sin the simple awareness of his dignity. This theory, on the contrary, found a place for the pride of the prince of the angels, while still respecting the rightness of his judgement. Satan, on this hypothesis, was in very truth proud, since he was vexed to see the privilege of hypostatic union given to another. His pride had for its object divinity itself: thus he was indeed he of whom Isaiah spoke. And this Satan, who desired to be God, was not the madman imagined by the old theologians. He desired divinity, but in a way which had nothing impossible in it, since he wished simply to be taken by the Word and form with Him a single personality, while yet preserving his separate nature. Suarez, struck by all these points, adopted the new theory and declared that, in his opinion, the sin of the Devil came from his desire to be taken himself by the Word as a term of the hypostatic union, instead of the human nature of Christ being that term.

This most seductive theory had only one fault, but

---

[1] Catharinus' theory: *De gloria bonorum angelorum et lapsu malorum.*

that a grave fault ; it was fantastic, and reposed upon no foundation ; or, what comes to the same thing, it rested upon an absolutely ruinous foundation. It based itself, it is true, upon an hypothesis given vogue by Alexander of Hales, according to which the Incarnation would have taken place even if man had not sinned. And, in fact, if this hypothesis is once admitted, it is quite natural to conclude that God had revealed to the angels, from the beginning, the project of incarnation, whose accomplishment was to take place in the course of the ages. But precisely this interpretation of Christ's coming was unknown to tradition. There was agreement that Christ was come to blot out the sins of men : these sins were regarded as the cause of the Incarnation, and there was no suspicion that the Word would have come upon earth apart from the Fall. Now evidently this traditional doctrine leaves no place for the explanation of Satan's sin proposed by Suarez. First of all, how could the Devil have had, before his fall, knowledge of a mystery which was not to be discovered save after the sin of Adam and, in consequence, after the fall of Satan himself, since our first father was led into temptation by the angel of darkness. Besides, Satan being a pure spirit, could not die. He was, therefore, incapable of redeeming mankind, and he could not delude himself on this point. Consequently, the desire to be chosen as the subject of the hypostatic union would have been as extravagant on his part as the desire to possess divinity.

In fine, to admit the explanation of Satan's sin so warmly recommended by Suarez, it was necessary first to adopt a theory of the mystery of the Incarnation in opposition to the teaching of the Fathers. Such a condition could not be accepted by all. The Scotists accepted it, and attributed the fall of the Devil to the unsatisfied desire for hypostatic union. The Thomists, on the other hand, remained attached, for lack of anything better, to the explanations that Suarez had so copiously refuted.

PART TWO

MALEVOLENT ACTIVITIES OF THE DEVIL IN HEAVEN

CHAPTER IV

THE ACTIVITY OF THE DEVIL IN HEAVEN
WAS NULL BEFORE ORIGEN

SINCE his fall, the former prince of the heavenly spirits has used his power only for evil. It was among the inhabitants of heaven that he made his first ravages ; it is in their ranks that his evil activity was first deployed.

But let us note this ; the discovery of this point in his history came late, and the Fathers were long in discovering that the wicked angels had been led into evil by Satan.

This brings us to the *Book of Enoch*. We know its interpretation of the text of *Genesis* which tells us of the marriage of the ' Sons of God ' with the daughters of men, and we know that, according to it, these ' Sons of God ' were angels. Let us add here this further information, which the same book provides us, in xii. 3, where we learn that the married angels were cursed by God :

> ' And I, Enoch, was blessing the Lord of Majesty and the King of the Ages, and lo! the Watchers called me, Enoch the Scribe, and said to me : Enoch, thou scribe of righteousness, go, declare to the Watchers of the heaven, who have left the high heaven, and have defiled themselves

29

with women, and have done as the children of the
earth do, and have taken unto themselves wives :
Ye have wrought great destruction on the earth ;
And ye shall have no peace nor forgiveness of
sin. . . .'

The *Book of Enoch*, which the *Epistle of Jude* (14)
cites as an authority, enjoyed great prestige. It was
of it that the first Fathers asked the secret of the
origin of demons and, at the same time, the interpretation of the famous text of *Genesis* vi. 2. Justin
is evidently inspired by Enoch in the text we have
already seen, where he speaks of the commerce of
angels with women. Irenæus relates to us (4, 16, 2)
that Enoch was charged by God to reprove the sinful
angels. He deduces this from the text above. The
Book of Enoch is thus, for him, an authority whose
ideas he accepts. Besides, all kind of doubt disappears
before 4, 36, 4, where we read that, at the time of
Noah : ' the sinful angels mingled with men.'
Irenæus believes in the commerce of wicked angels
with women. Clement of Alexandria (*The Instructor*,
3, 2) quotes, in order to turn men away from concupiscence, the example of the

> ' angels who abandoned the beauty of God, turned
> towards an ephemeral beauty and fell from heaven
> to earth.'

Elsewhere (*Stromates*, 5, 1), Clement shows us the
angels, carried away by evil passions, in intimate con-
verse with the women, to whom they reveal secrets.

Tertullian, in order to inspire women with a horror
of adornments, says to them (*De cultu feminarum*,

1, 2), that those who invented these vanities were condemned to death. Then he describes these inventors :

' They were the angels who hurled themselves from heaven towards the daughters of men, as if women were not sufficiently outraged (they taught men the secrets of nature) ; to women they taught, above all, how to profit by adorning themselves. . . . Why did they give them these lessons ? Was it because, without all the attraction of ornaments, women would be incapable of pleasing men ? No, since without the aid of any ornament, their simple natural beauty had been able to seduce the angels . . ."

Tertullian here explains that the angels loaded their spouses with ornaments, to make them incur the anger of God. In another book (*De virginibus velondis*, 7) the same doctor assures us that the angels slaked their passion not upon married women, but upon virgins. He takes as the basis of his argument a text from the *First Epistle to the Corinthians* xi. 10, where we read that women ought to wear a veil ' because of the angels.' He says :

' If women ought to wear a veil because of the angels who, as we read, for the love of women lost God and heaven, who would believe that these angels, instead of choosing virgins to feed their concupiscence, took bodies already defiled, the remains of human voluptuousness ? . . . Therefore so dangerous a beauty ought to be veiled, for it has caused ravages even in heaven. . . .'

Saint Cyprian, too, like Tertullian, and with formulæ in part borrowed from Tertullian, wants to turn women away from luxury ; he says, speaking of adornment (*De habitu virginum*, 14) :

> ' It is the sinful and apostate angels who, by their artifices, taught all these things when, overcome by the contagious influence of human charms, they lost the power which they had in heaven.'

SATAN TEMPTS JESUS

Engraving by Johann Sadler, 1582, in the Cabinet des
Estampes de La Bibliothèque Nationale

CHAPTER V

THE ACTIVITY OF THE DEVIL WAS EVIL
AFTER ORIGEN

WE have seen that the first Fathers did not mingle the fall of the Devil with the fall of the demons. According to them, the evil angels let themselves be seduced, not by the prince of the heavenly court, but by their own passions. Supplementary information was needed for the alteration of this judgement and to implicate Satan in the catastrophe, to which he had at first been thought a stranger.

The additional information was supplied by Origen's metaphysic. We know this philosophy, for which the material world is the result of what, in chemistry, is called an oxidation; an oxidation produced by sin. All the bodies of which our universe is composed serve to imprison the guilty spirits. They did not exist while these spirits kept to the right way. It is thus nonsense to attribute the sin of the angels to the love of women. Origen rejects as a fable the tale of the *Book of Enoch*. He considers as allegory the text of *Genesis* vi. 2, of which the account of Enoch is a paraphrase. Then he teaches that the angels sinned before the existence of the world, by acts of which we are ignorant.[1]

---

[1] *Contra Celsum*, 5, 54–55; *De Principiis*, 1, 8, 4.

Thus, according to Origen, the demons sinned before the existence of the world, and they sinned by acts of which we know nothing. Let us see what became of these two assertions. The first found only one gainsayer in the East, Methodus to wit, who remained in the track of Justin and Clement of Alexandria. Apart from Methodus, the Greek Church marched resolutely along the way opened up by its great doctor. Certain words of Saint Chrysostom lead us to suspect that the old doctrine still had partisans among the people at the end of the fourth century. In any case, Chrysostom rejects it with scorn. He explains to his audience that the ' Sons of God' of whom *Genesis* vi. 2 speaks, are men, and that the angels have never been able to have carnal commerce with women.[1]

Origen's reforms found it harder to penetrate the West. Lactantius was completely ignorant of them. He continued to relate, like Justin, that several of the guardian angels, charged by God with watching over the world, sinned with women and engendered children. One would expect Saint Ambrose to be less chained to tradition. Ambrose read Origen and he liked him ; he is one of those who initiated the West into Origen's ideas. Yet he said, he too, that the angels did have carnal commerce with women.[2] Saint Hilary and Saint Jerome profited more, upon this point, from the master's lessons. They refused to bow down before the authority of the *Book of*

---

[1] Homily upon *Genesis*, 22, 2 ; see also Theodoret, *Hieretica fabulæ*, 5, 7.
[2] *De virginibus*, 1, 52; *De Noe et Arca*, 8.

Enoch, and showed that they did not accept its theory of the fall of the demons.

Saint Augustine was greatly perplexed. The opinion of the first Fathers was not unknown to him. We read, in the *City of God*, 15, 22 :

> ' Many believe that the sons of God of whom *Genesis* speaks were angels and not men.'

When he wrote that, Augustine was thinking, doubtless, of Tertullian, Saint Cyprian and Saint Ambrose, his masters. And, besides, daily experience favoured this opinion. Augustine adds :

> ' It is recounted everywhere that satyrs and fauns frequently unite with women. Certain demons, whom the Gauls call *Duses*, are specially accused of this crime. And tales of this nature are so numerous and so well authorised that it would, in my opinion, be presumptuous to reject them.'

On the other hand, he saw those whom he called ' prudent men '—obviously Saint Hilary and Saint Jerome—refuse any kind of authority to the *Book of Enoch*. Further, he had procured, upon the occasion of the Pelagian controversy, the *Homilies* of Saint Chrysostom, and in them he had seen that the ' Sons of God ' of *Genesis* were to be considered as men. What was he to do, in this conflict of authorities and arguments ? Augustine decided, not without pain, to abandon the old opinion and to ascribe to men the adventure recounted in *Genesis*. Nevertheless, the tales relative to incubus demons had produced a profound impression on his mind. He could not refuse to spirits, provided with an aerial body, the power of feeling passion for women and uniting themselves with them.

Augustine would have been able by his own sole authority to drive out from the Latin Church the doctrine that Tertullian, Cyprian and Ambrose had professed. He had, moreover, an auxiliary in Cassian. A disciple of Jerome at Bethlehem and of Chrysostom at Constantinople, Cassian knew how to profit by the teaching of his masters. In his *Collationes* he employed, when speaking of the angels, almost the same terms as Chrysostom. Thanks to him, Origen's teaching spread in the monastic world and, from there, throughout the whole Church. Sulpicius Severus, it is true, remained attached to the school of Tertullian. That was because he was a contemporary of Augustine, and because the voice of the great doctor of the Latin Church had not been able to reach him. After Sulpicius Severus, the Latin Church renounced, like the Greek Church, its attempt to find in licentiousness the explanation of the fall of the demons.

The demons were not led into evil by lewdness. How, then, did they fall? Origen provided no light on this point. But Eusebius teaches us that Satan made the other angels fall. The same assertion reappears in Gregory of Nazianzus.[1] We read in Saint Chrysostom that the demons, like the Devil, desired to raise themselves above their condition.[2] Following

---

[1] *Poemata theologica*, 7, 69.
[2] *Homilies upon Genesis*, 22, 2.

Chrysostom's example, Saint Augustine attributed the fall of the angels to pride.[1] This view had a great success. The author of the *Letter to Demetriades* (probably Saint Leo) also spoke of pride, and from then on, none spoke otherwise.

[1] *Enchiridion*, 28.

CHAPTER VI

SCRIPTURAL PROOF OF THE INFLUENCE
OF THE DEVIL

FROM the middle of the fourth century onwards,
Satan was known as the author of the fall of the
demons. Upon what did this knowledge rest? Its
basis was, at first, purely logical. The Devil appeared
in the New Testament as chief of the army of the
demons. It was natural to associate with his fall that
of his subordinates, and to combine it all into one
whole. The first Fathers, it is true, could not achieve
this operation. They were stopped by the *Book of
Enoch*, which placed the fall of the demons in the
time of Noah and attributed it to lewdness, while
Genesis showed our first parents as the victims of the
Devil's jealousy. But, from the day when Origen
relegated Enoch's account to the fables, and trans-
posed Satan's sin to before the appearance of the
human race, logic resumed its rights, and its demands
could be listened to. This is how Eusebius and Saint
Gregory of Nazianzus were led to connect the fall of
the demons with that of the Devil.

A Scriptural text alone was able, here as elsewhere, to establish the demands of logic beyond
contestation. The text that was needed was discovered by Saint Jerome. In chapter xii. of the

Apocalypse, a dragon is described whose tail sweeps a third of the stars of heaven, and against whom Michael, helped by his angels, wages a victorious war. Jerome recognised in this text a description of the fall of Satan, and he perceived that the stars swept by the tail of the dragon were the wicked angels who, at the beginning of time, had shared in the revolt of the prince of the heavenly court. At that time he was engaged in remodelling the *Commentary* of Victorinus upon the *Apocalypse:* he inserted his discovery into this.[1] Cassian profited by Jerome's exegesis. In his *Collationes*, 8, after mentioning the fall of the Devil, he added :

'Scripture says that the dragon drew after him in his fall a third of the stars.'

In his *Commentary upon the Apocalypse*, Cassiodorus explained, following Cassian, that Michael's combat against the dragon

'took place incontestably at the beginning of the world.'

Before going any further, let us look back again and see how the doctors of the first three centuries interpreted this scene of the dragon in the *Apocalypse*.

[1] Migne, *Patr. lat.*, 5, 536 : 'Many think that the third of the stars seduced by the tail of the dragon represents a third of all the Christians. The truth is that the dragon seduced a third of the angels, who were under his orders when he was the first of them.' This text is that of Saint Jerome, who has here corrected Victorinus' version. He also presented the same interpretation in his *Commentary on Psalm* lxxxi., 7 (*Anecdota Maredsoliana*, 3, 2, 18), where, having spoken of the fall of the Devil from Heaven, he adds: 'Read the *Apocalypse* of Saint John : there we read that, on the day when the dragon fell from heaven, he drew after him in his fall a third of the stars.'

Irenæus, who mentions it in 2, 31, 2, sees in it a prophetic description of the misdeeds of the heretics of his time : thus he places it in the future. Hippolytus [1] does not think otherwise : for him, chapter xii. of the *Apocalypse* is a picture of the persecutions inflicted on the Church by the Devil. And Origen used the same expressions.[2] In fact, during the first three centuries, the passage of the dragon passed for a prophecy of the trials of the Church, and Saint Jerome's interpretation rebelled against tradition.

This explains the views which we have still to survey. Saint Gregory the Great, speaking of the tail of the dragon, explains that the heaven where dwell the stars swept by the tail is the Church, and that the stars are the Christians, of whom Satan makes sinners by leading them into evil. As for the intervention of Saint Michael, it will take place, according to him, at the end of the world, in order to precipitate Satan into hell.[3] Bede reproduces the views of Saint Gregory.[4] Alcuin thinks that Saint Michael's combat is fulfilled in the struggles with which the whole history of the Church is filled.[5] Strabo, Haymon, Rupert use similar language.[6] As we see, during the whole of the early Middle Ages, the passage of the dragon of the *Apocalypse* was, with rare exceptions, interpreted according to the thought of the first

---

[1] *De Christo et Antichristo*, 60.

[2] *In Matth.*, 23, 49.

[3] *Morals*, 32, 251, and *Homilies upon the Gospels*, 34, 9.

[4] *Commentary upon the Apocalypse*, 12, 4.

[5] *Ibid.*

[6] Strabo, in his *Gloss*, Migne, 114, 732 ; Haymon, Migne, 117, 108, 1089 ; Rupert, Migne, 169, 1051. (According to Rupert, the fallen stars are the apostate Jews.)

Fathers, and Saint Jerome's interpretation, which was rejected by Saint Gregory the Great, was also rejected by nearly all the commentators.

It was reserved for Petrus Lombardus to reverse the situation. Petrus did not want to deprive himself of the services of so precious an interpretation and, regardless of tradition, he proved by the passage of the dragon in the *Apocalypse* that Satan had perverted a portion of the angels.[1] Saint Thomas followed Petrus Lombardus. His attitude was decisive.[2] From that time on, nearly all the theologians based their doctrine of the leading astray of the wicked angels by Satan upon the *Apocalypse*. Suarez, who was aware of the difficulty of the problem, solved it in a very ingenious manner.[3] He says :

> 'It cannot be denied that the first sense (that which applies the text to the events at the end of the world) is the more literal. But, all the same, the second may have been intended by the Holy Spirit, either in the spiritual sense or in a secondary literal sense.'

A theologian worthy of the name is competent to find his way out of any *impasse!*

[1] *Sententiae*, 2, 6, 2.

[2] *Summa*, 1, 63, 8. Saint Thomas' master, Albertus Magnus (*In Sententias*, 2, 6, 3, end), refuses to follow Petrus Lombardus, and remains faithful to the traditional interpretation.

[3] *De Angelis*, 7, 17, 20.

CHAPTER VII

THE PROPORTIONATE NUMBER OF THE DEMONS

THE doctors have never fixed, even approximately, the absolute number of the demons. What they have managed to determine is, the proportion of the number of demons compared with the good angels. Hugo St Victor, the first who put the question, conjectured at random that the fallen angels were in a minority compared with the faithful angels. But he admitted that he was unable to support his opinion by any authority. Saint Thomas, who never liked to remain in doubt, pronounced categorically for the smaller number of the damned angels.[1] His decision was motivated by the principle that sin, being contrary to nature, is an exception. The opinion of the angelic doctor had the force of law. Nevertheless, it was impossible not to observe that proof lacked. It amounted, in fact, to demonstrating, contrary to the facts, that sin is an exception in the human race. Hence, efforts were made to correct it or, at least, to complete it; and it was agreed that the principle according to which sin is contrary to the inclination of nature does not apply to the human nature that has become vitiated since

[1] Hugo, *De Sacramentis*, 1, 5, 31; Saint Thomas, *Summa*, 1, 63, 9.

Adam's fall.[1] Suarez, even, completely rejected the proof.[2] According to him God, whose infinite knowledge knows all possibilities, could, if He had so wished, have created only those angels whom He foresaw would remain faithful. He could, conversely, have created only those angels whom He foresaw would sin. Suarez concluded that, if the minority only of the heavenly spirits had fallen, the final reason for this must be sought in the divine Providence which decided thus.

The Devil made great carnage on high; he ravished from heaven a notable portion of its inhabitants. Now he is going to continue his sinister exploits on earth. Before we follow him to this new theatre, let us pause to inform ourselves concerning the conditions of existence laid down for him and for his army. What is the nature of the Devil and of the demons? Where is their actual dwelling-place? What is their destiny—that which they have to undergo to-day, and that which awaits them after the end of the world? These are all points which we must clear up.

[1] Estius, *In Sententias*, 2, 6, 11.
[2] Suarez, *De angelis*, 7, 17, 10.

CHAPTER VIII

THE DEVIL AND THE DEMONS WERE,
AT FIRST, CORPOREAL BEINGS

THE Devil and the demons are, like the good
angels, pure spirit-beings, that is to say, beings
into whom no material element enters, and whom
the laws of space do not affect. But in the Latin
Church they did not possess this prerogative until
the twelfth century. It is the same, as a matter
of fact, with the good angels. Before this date, all
the angels, good and bad had, in the opinion of
the doctors of the West, ethereal or aerial bodies.
Doubtless, they were called spirits, but this term did
not then have the rigorous sense that philosophy has
given it. Indeed, the nature of the Devil and of the
demons has, in the course of the centuries, undergone
a profound evolution, in which the nature of the good
angels has also participated. Let us give proof for
this assertion.

All the doctors who have explained the fall of the
bad angels by lewdness necessarily attribute to them
organs analogous to our own, for it is clear that pure
spirit-beings cannot be touched by voluptuousness.
This simple observation guides us as to the thought
of Justin, Irenæus, Clement of Alexandria, and Tertullian. It shows us that all these doctors, and others

too, conceived the angels as beings of an ethereal or aerial nature, but in any case a material one. And, besides, our induction is confirmed by decisive texts.

Justin explains, in the *Dialogue*, 57, 2, that the angels nourish themselves in heaven with food. He adds that their food consists of manna; which he proves by the text of *Psalms* (lxxviii. 25), where it is said that the Israelites in the desert ate the bread of the angels. However, he adds that the angels have not, like us, teeth and jaws, but that they absorb their food by devouring it, as fire devours combustibles. Clement of Alexandria (*The Instructor*, 1, 6), and Tertullian (*Upon the Flesh of Christ*, 6), utilise the above text from the *Psalms*; they declare that Hebrews, when they ate manna, were feeding upon the ordinary food of the angels. In his book, *Contra Marcionem*, 2, 8, Tertullian says that the food of the angels is made of an aery material, and he proves his assertion by the aid of *Psalm* ciii. 4 (already quoted by the author of *To the Hebrews*), where we read that God uses the winds as angels, that is to say, as messengers. In the same book (3, 9), he says that the elect, on the day of Resurrection, will be clothed with ' the true angelic substance,' in other words, that our bodies will be similar to those of the angels. He calls the angels spiritual substances (*Upon the Flesh of Christ*, 6), but he explains that this name is suitable to them because they have a body of a particular kind.[1]

[1] Irenæus says (3, 20, 4) that the angels have no flesh, but Massuet himself (*Dissertatio*, 3, 8, 102) recognises that this expression in no way implies belief in the absolute spirituality of the angels. Besides, Irenæus accepts the account of *Enoch*.

We know that, according to Origen, the heavenly spirits alone existed in God's first plan, and that the world as it is was made to serve as a prison for the guilty angels. That being so, we might think that the absolute spirituality of the angels was introduced into the Church by this doctor. Nothing of the kind. Origen attributed a material envelope to all the spirits : and, in so doing, he did not think he was making a more or less probable conjecture ; he was drawing the inference from his philosophical principles.[1] Like the Stoic school, in fact, he conceived matter as a principle of individuation, as the envelope which isolates one spiritual being from another and prevents them from melting together. According to him, the Divine Persons escape from this law because of their superiority, and their intrinsic excellence. Dominating the created spirits so greatly, they are not exposed to confusion with them. They can, therefore, subsist without a material envelope. But with the spirits it is quite otherwise. Being all of the same nature, they cannot subsist and preserve their independence save by means of matter. Oil in contact with water is superposed upon it ; but two drops of water would mix together and would lose their individuality if nothing held them back. Whence this phrase, which we read in the treatise *De Principiis*, 1, 6, 4 :

'It is impossible for me to understand how so many substances can live without a body. God alone, that is to say, the Father, the Son and the

[1] Denis, *La Philosophie d'Origène*, pp. 170–77.

Holy Spirit, can exist without the aid of a material substance.'

Yet Origen teaches that our world owes its existence to the fall of the spirits. But that which he considers as posterior to the fall, that which, according to him, was produced by the sin of the angels, was the gross matter of our world. This matter is posterior to the fall of the angels; to speak more exactly, it was only produced to receive the spirits fallen from their primitive condition (*ibid.*, 2, 1, 1); but it is itself only a transformation of a subtle, light and shining matter which existed in the beginning. It was not drawn from out the void; it was the former matter condensed. Listen to Origen (*ibid.*, 4, 35):

'God, foreseeing that reasonable nature would be unstable, made matter transformable, so that each spirit should have a corporeal envelope corresponding to his deserts.'

In other words, spirits all had, from the beginning, a subtle substance; according to whether they sinned more or less, this matter has become, so to speak, oxidised and corrupt, and has become the body of a man, a quadruped, or a fish.

Origen alone would have been able, in the third century, to modify accepted opinions about the constitution of the angelic world. His ideas were long to remain in the Church. Saint Cyril of Jerusalem calls the demons spirits; but he is careful to explain (*Catecheses*, 16, 15) that the name spirit is given to any being who has not a gross body.[1] Saint Basil, in two or three places, attributes a spiritual nature to the angels and to the Devil. But when he expresses his thought in detail he says (*De spiritu sancto*, 38) :

> 'The substance of the heavenly Virtues is an airy breath or an immaterial flame of fire, as it is written : "He maketh winds his messengers, his ministers a flaming fire."'

Saint Ambrose, in his book *Concerning Abraham*, 2, 58, says :

> 'We consider that no being is exempt from material composition, save the substance of the venerable Trinity.'

Saint Augustine shows us his conception of the angels in texts of limpid clearness. In his *Homily upon Psalm* lxxxv. 17, we read :

> 'Our present body, compared with the body which we shall one day have, compared with the body of the angels, is dead, although it possesses a soul.'

When he speaks of the body which we shall receive after the Last Judgement, he says indifferently that this body will be spiritual, celestial, angelic, that it will be the body of an angel. He says, for instance, in *Sermon*, 45, 10 :

> 'Just as our mortal flesh will be transformed into the body of an angel, so will our tears be turned into rejoicing.'

[1] See Touttee's note on 16, 15, which proves that Cyril attributed subtle and ethereal bodies to the angels.

SATAN IS SPEARED BY JESUS WHO IS DESCENDING INTO HELL

Parement de Narbonne in the Louvre

Having to explain how, after the Resurrection, we shall be able to see thoughts, he says (*Book of Eighty-three Questions*, 9, 47):

'We must believe that the angelic bodies, that is, the bodies which we hope to have, are luminous and ethereal. If then we can actually read thoughts in the eyes, it is probable that, when our body is ethereal, no thought will remain hidden.'

What do the angels do to make themselves visible to men? Augustine gives two explanations. Sometimes he thinks that for this the angels have only to thicken their natural bodies; sometimes he hesitates and asks himself if the natural body of the angels can transform itself, or if these bodies, remaining invisible, are not clothed with a body borrowed for the occasion from our gross matter. The first solution appears in *Sermon*, 12, 9:

'The angels, although they are not born of woman, have, nevertheless, received a true body, which it is in their power to transform, in such a way as to give it this or that appearance, according to the exigencies of their ministry.'

On the other hand, we read in the *De Trinitate*, 3, 5:

'I confess that I cannot decide whether, their spiritual bodies remaining what they are, the angels borrow from the inferior elements the body which they put on like a garment and transform at will . . . or whether it is their own body which they thus transform.'

D

The same uncertainty exists in the *Enchiridion*, 59, written in 421, that is, about ten years after the *De Trinitate*. There is at least one thing of which Augustine is sure, and of which he never doubts : it is that the angels have a body which he calls spiritual, that is to say, ethereal.[1]

Cassian is far from attaining the genius of Augustine. But he exercised a considerable influence over the monks, which only disappeared with Saint Gregory the Great. Let us address ourselves to him. This is what he says (*Collatio*, 8, 13) :

> ' When we proclaim that there are spiritual natures such as the angels, the archangels, the other virtues, our souls and the subtle air, we must not think that they are incorporeal. They have a body which makes them subsist ; but this body is much more subtle than ours.'

Thus, according to Cassian, the angel is a spiritual nature ; but the subtle air is another. And, whether we consider it in the air or in the angel, this spiritual nature is, nevertheless, corporeal.

Now let us transport ourselves to the Middle Ages. In the ninth century Scotus Erigena asserts that the demons had before their fall an ethereal body and that, following their fall, an aerial body was superposed upon the primitive ethereal one. Florus combats this assertion (*Contre Scot Erigène*, 17, 5 ; Migne, 119, 222). But why ? Florus is indignant with Scotus

---

[1] See also the *De divinatione dæmonum*, 7, where Augustine explains that the demons, thanks to their aerial body, have an extraordinary agility and power of perception.

Erigena's temerity in being positive where Augustine did not dare pronounce judgement, and in attributing to the demons two bodies superposed, whereas perhaps they have no other body than their primitive body condensed. We conclude that Florus, one of the doctors of the ninth century, attributed an ethereal body to the good angels and an aerial body to the demons.

Three centuries later it was the same. Honoré of Autun says in his book *Of the Twelve Questions*, 11 (Migne, 172, 1183):

> ' The angels have ethereal bodies, the demons have aereal bodies, men have terrestrial bodies. The bodies of the angels are simple, that is to say, made of pure ether. Ether is fire, that is to say, the fourth element.'

Rupert writes (*De Victoria Verbi Dei*, 1, 28; Migne, 169, 1841):

> ' With what were the angels made ? With the substance of the air. They have aereal bodies . . . however, these bodies have, in the holy angels, undergone a happy transformation . . . as a result of which they have become celestial bodies.'

Petrus Lombardus is perplexed (*Sententiæ*, 2, 8). He begins by setting forth the opinion, according to which the angels had, in the beginning, aerial bodies, which were transformed later, in the faithful angels, into ethereal bodies, and in the demons into grosser bodies. Then he observes that Augustine seemed to have been of this opinion; and having given a text

from this great doctor, he cannot prevent himself
from concluding that :

> 'Augustine does indeed seem to teach what
> some say concerning the bodies of the angels.'

However, impartiality obliges him to tell us that
there is another opinion, and how the representatives
of this opinion use the texts of Saint Augustine to
serve them :

> 'Others assert that, when he spoke thus, Augus-
> tine did not give his own opinion, but confined
> himself to relating the opinion of others.'

Petrus does not here tell us what he thinks of this
scapeway, and he maintains the most absolute reserve.
But he cannot keep this attitude for long. A little
later, in fact, having to explain how the angels make
themselves visible to men, he relates the two hypotheses of Augustine, that according to which the
angels condense their ethereal bodies and that which
makes them clothe themselves with a material body
over their ethereal body. After citing these texts,
Petrus is careful to set in relief the precise point upon
which the uncertainty of the great doctor is directed,
and he concludes by saying :

> 'By these words, Augustine seems to confirm
> that the angels are corporeal, and that they have
> spiritual bodies properly belonging to them.'

This phrase is his final word, wherein the master of
the *Sententiæ* unveils his thought to us, which till
then he had kept hidden. Petrus is evidently convinced that Saint Augustine attributes a body to the

angels. And, as Augustine is, by predilection, his master, he himself does not conceive the angelic world otherwise. But he takes into account that the fashion is different and that, if he took up a militant attitude, he would come into direct opposition with the common opinion. Therefore, he keeps his opinion without seeking to impose it.

CHAPTER IX

THE DEVIL AND THE DEMONS ARE, TO-DAY,
PURE SPIRIT-BEINGS

At the epoch when Petrus Lombardus was writing his *Sententiæ*, the Devil—and with him the whole angelic world—was in process of transformation. The ethereal or aerial body which, up till then, he had possessed, was in process of vanishing. The Devil was becoming a pure spirit-being. And Petrus Lombardus who, out of respect for Saint Augustine, retained this body, is a belated conservative. He closes an era while another is, despite him, beginning. He is not absolutely alone in taking up this reactionary attitude. In his company we note Saint Bernard who, he too, would like to remain faithful to tradition. For this is what we read in his book, *De Consideratione*, 5, 4, 7 :

> ' The angels have ethereal bodies. . . . There are, I know, doctors who ask themselves, not only whence come the angelic bodies, but even if these bodies exist. If anyone wishes to regard this point as among arguable opinions, I shall not cavil.'

Bernard, like Petrus Lombardus, is attached to antiquity, and he conceals but ill the contempt with which the innovators inspire him.

Who are these innovators? Dennis the Areopagite and Hugo St Victor. They did not live at the
same time and their rôles differed. One was the
initiator and the other the populariser. Let us
examine these two men.

At the beginning of the sixth century there
appeared the book *Of the Heavenly Hierarchy*.[1] It
says that the angelic world is divided into three hier-
archies, each of which comprises three orders. It
says also that the angels are beings, simple, without
shape, and that the sensible forms under which they
are represented are symbols, and that it would be an
error to attribute to the angels material properties,
however noble and brilliant. The author of this
book, to which three other books, notably *Of
the Divine Names*, were added, entitled himself
Dennis the Areopagite, converted by Saint Paul
at Athens. In reality, he was a Neoplatonist, im-
bued with the doctrines of Plotinus and, above
all, of Proclus. The book, which revolutionised
the status of the angels in general and of the Devil
in particular, was the work of a forger. Put forward and exploited by the Monophysites, it was at
first rejected by the Catholics as apocryphal. But
this opposition did not persist. By the middle of
the sixth century the book *Of the Heavenly Hierarchy* was attributed in Catholic circles to a disciple
of Saint Paul. From this time on, the absolute
spirituality of the angels began to penetrate the
Eastern Church, where it was to be propagated,

[1] See, upon the Areopagite, the works of Koch and of the Jesuit
Stilmayer, published in 1895.

two centuries later, under the influence of Saint John of Damascus.

In the West, Saint Gregory the Great who, during his sojourn at Constantinople, had become acquainted with the Areopagite books, used them as a source in his writings. Further, in the ninth century, Scotus Erigena translated, at the command of Charles the Bald, the above-mentioned books, of which a Greek copy had reached the court of the Carolingian emperors. Thus circumstances seemed favourable. But the laconic texts of Gregory were not noticed. As for Scotus Erigena, he was such an object of horror that for long no one would read his work. We have to come to Hugo St Victor to see the situation alter. Hugo read *The Heavenly Hierarchy;* he wrote a commentary upon it which has come down to us ; he was filled through and through with its doctrines. He is a decided partisan of the absolute spirituality of the angels. He teaches that the angelic substance is simple and immaterial. He even takes care to explain to us that the heavenly spirits were not fashioned with a pre-existing matter, as were the material creatures.[1] It was he who introduced into the Latin Church the system of the Areopagite. It is, thanks to him, that the Devil and all the angels obtained their rights in scholasticism as pure spirit-beings.

For Hugo made proselytes. Saint Bernard and Petrus Lombardus testify to his influence when they admit, not without grief, that tradition has been pierced and broken by a modernist thrust. One of

[1] *De Sacramentis,* I, 5, 7–8.

the first disciples of Hugo was Richard St Victor. This partisan of the absolute spirituality of the angels gave a proof of it which deserves to be noted. It is based on the story of the demoniac in the Gospels, in whose body a legion of demons had taken up residence. Richard begins by noting that a legion consists of 6666 individuals. Next he demonstrates without difficulty the absolute impossibility of a man's body lodging so many guests. He adds (*De Trinitate*, 5, 25):

'Do not say that the angelic spirits, the good like the bad, have subtle bodies. For, however subtle they be, these bodies cannot interpenetrate. What smallness will you attribute to them in order to lodge so many angelic bodies in the skin of one man?'

In spite of his authority, Petrus Lombardus could not stop the current of sympathy which drew toward Hugo. Even those who commentated his *Sententiæ*, who professed to be his disciples, Alexander of Hales, Albertus Magnus, Saint Thomas, Saint Bonaventure, pronounced in favour of the absolute spirituality of the angelic world. We read in Albertus (*In Sententias*, 2, 8, 1):

'The Fathers have given forth divers hypotheses on this subject. But to-day the light is full, and we understand that Augustine did not present his own opinion, but that of others. In consequence, we cannot doubt that the angels are spiritual substances.'

A few lines before, Albertus informs us who are

those who brought the light to bear upon the nature
of the heavenly spirits. They are Dennis the Areopagite and Saint John Damascenus.

As for Saint Thomas, he does not delay to cite his
authorities. He transports us at once into the regions
of metaphysics (*Summa*, 1, 50, 1). There he explains
to us that the motive for which the Supreme Being
draws forth creatures from the void is the good ; that
the good consists in resemblance to God ; that, in
order to resemble God perfectly, the creature must
participate in the Creator's mode of action, that is to
say, have an intelligence and a will of his own, since
God acts by the intelligence and the will. This great
doctor observes, in this connection, that the intelligence and the will are faculties of an immaterial order;
then he concludes :

> 'In order that the universe be perfect, it is
> necessary to admit an incorporeal creature.'

The question was to know whether the angels were
spiritual, or had bodies. We learn, not only that their
nature is spiritual, but that that is a necessary thing,
and could not have been otherwise.

The absolute spirituality of the angels had already
put forth profound roots in theology before Saint
Thomas. The author of the *Summa* fortified it yet
further and gave it an unshakable position. From
the middle of the thirteenth century, the theory
formulated by the Areopagite became an incontro-
vertible truth. To speak exactly, it did still encounter
two or three opponents, like Cajetan,[1] who gives

[1] *In Epistol. ad Ephesios*, 2, 2.

aerial bodies to the demons, and Sixtus of Sienna,[1] who declines to know more about the angels than Saint Bernard had done. But these obstinate conservatives seemed extravagant. The doctrine that had reigned during the first five centuries was definitely abandoned.

[1] *Bibliotheca sancta*, 5, 8.

CHAPTER X

THE DOMICILE OF THE DEVIL AND THE DEMONS

THE *Book of Enoch* devotes two groups of texts to the sojourn of the guilty angels and of their posterity. One[1] tells us that the angels seduced by the women are, from now on, enchained beneath the hills of the earth and that later, on the Day of Judgement, they will be hurled into the abyss of fire. The second (15, 8-12), speaking of the beings issued from the commerce of the angels with the women, assigns to these as domicile the earth, where they strive to injure mankind.

The *Epistle of Jude* speaks in these terms of the guilty angels (6) :

> 'And angels, which kept not their own principality, but left their proper habitation, he hath kept in everlasting bonds under darkness unto the judgement of the great day.'

The same doctrine appears in the *Second Epistle of Peter* (ii. 4) :

> 'For God spared not angels when they sinned, but cast them down to hell, and committed them to pits of darkness, to be reserved unto judgement.'

[1] See 10, 4–6, whose doctrine reappears with variations in 10, 11–13 ; 21, 7–10 ; 54, 5–6.

And in the *Apocalypse* (xx. 2-3) there is a description of an angel who

" laid hold on the dragon, the old serpent, which is the Devil and Satan, and bound him for a thousand years, and cast him into the abyss, and shut it and sealed it over him, that he should deceive the nations no more, until the thousand years should be finished.'

All these texts are obviously inspired by the *Book of Enoch*, whose thought they sometimes modify. But the New Testament does not give the same view throughout. For instance, the *Epistle to the Ephesians* ii. 2, says that the Christians, before their conversion, lived

' According to the prince of the power of the air, of the spirit that now worketh in the sons of disobedience.'

In the *First Epistle of Peter* (v. 8) we read that :

' The Devil as a roaring lion walketh about, seeking whom he may devour.'

And in the Gospel of *St John* there is mention several times (xii. 31 ; xiv. 30 ; xv. 11) of the ' Prince of this world.' These formulæ state or suppose that the Devil has his dwelling-place in the air, whence he presides over the course of the world.

The Fathers were obliged to take into account the teachings provided by the *Apocalypse*, by *Jude*, and by the *Second Epistle of St Peter*. But neither could they neglect the texts that placed the Devil's domicile in the air. And besides, the Greek philosophy, into which they were all more or less initiated, was based upon this phrase of Heraclitus, reported by Diogenes Laertius : [1]

' All the parts of the world are filled with spirits and with demons.'

Thus hell claimed the Devil and his satellites. But our terrestrial atmosphere also had its pretensions to be their dwelling-place. How was this problem to be solved ? One of Christ's sayings, inserted about the middle of the second century in *St Matthew* (xxv. 41) explains that hell ' is prepared for the devil and his angels.' ' Prepared '—that is to say, that the Devil and his satellites will inhabit hell at the end of the world, but that they do not yet inhabit it. All the Fathers adhered to this explanation. They admitted that the Devil and the demons actually resided in the air ; but they added that this state of things would change at the end of the world, and that the diabolic army would then be hurled into hell, there to suffer the torture of fire. Whence it follows that the Enemy of God ranges freely through the air, and that, by himself or by his subordinates, he makes war upon mankind : but this provisional regime will one day be replaced by that of hell. This arrangement seemed to satisfy at the same time the *Apocalypse* and the *Epistle to the Ephesians :* it reconciled them.

A lame conciliation. For the texts of the *Apocalypse*, of *Jude*, and of the *Second Epistle of St Peter*

---

[1] Diogenes Laertius, *The Lives of the Most Illustrious Philosophers*, 9, 1.

do not limit themselves to referring to the sojourn of the Devil in hell. They say that this sojourn is an accomplished fact, and that the diabolic army has long, according to the words of the *Apocalypse*, 'been plunged into the abyss.' That was a great difficulty. But Saint Augustine, who perceived it, solved it magnificently. In the *City of God*, 20, 7, 3, the text of the *Apocalypse* is subjected to the following commentary :

'The abyss into which the Devil has been hurled is the innumerable multitude of the impious, whose hearts are, for the Church of God, abysses of hatred. Not that the Devil was not already there. But, excluded from possession of the faithful, he seized yet more firmly upon the impious.'

And, in the *Homily upon Psalm* cxlviii. 9, we read :

'The Devil was expelled at the same time as his angels from the exalted dwelling-place of the angels, and he was thrown into darkness, that is to say, into our atmosphere, as into prison. That is what the apostle teaches us in the *Epistle to the Ephesians*, where he speaks of the Prince of the Air. It is also what another apostle says when he tells us that God did not spare the guilty angels ; but that he imprisoned them in the shades of hell ; for what he calls hell is our earth, which is the lower part of the world.'

Thus we see that the Devil and the demons are, from now on, in the abyss, in hell. But as the abyss is constituted by the hearts of the impious, as hell means our atmosphere, the diabolic army is none the less in the air and upon earth. This time the conciliation leaves nothing to be desired; the *Apocalypse* is fully in accord with the *Epistle to the Ephesians.*

Saint Augustine's luminous explanation, which was accepted by Saint Gregory the Great,[1] was law until the middle of the twelfth century. At this time Petrus Lombardus undertook, timidly, to modify it. He continued to teach (*Sententiæ*, 2, 6, 2) that the demons are scattered throughout the shadowy air, and that our atmosphere is the prison spoken of in the *Second Epistle of Peter.* But he added (2, 6, 6) that Lucifer is perhaps already plunged into hell, and (5) that certain demons descend into it to accompany the souls of the damned. He says even:

> ' Some of them are probably there on permanent duty to torment the damned. Perhaps, too, they relieve one another, turn and turn about.'

Petrus Lombardus had given his assertion the value of a conjecture merely. Saint Thomas (*Summa*, 1, 64, 4) raised it to the degree of an absolute thesis. According to him, beside the demons who reside in the air, there are others who reside in hell, where they torment the damned. This opinion, favoured by the prince of theologians, became, little by little, a certitude. Since the sixteenth century, it is accepted that the rebel angels were hurled to the depths of hell immediately after their sin and that, later, certain

---

[1] *Morals*, 32, 10.

THE DEVIL ASSISTS AT THE WEIGHING OF SOULS
BY ST MICHAEL AT THE LAST JUDGEMENT
Centre part of the Last Judgement in the Cathedral at Bourges

amongst them were authorised to come into the air to harm mankind. The learned Melchior Cano proposed to leave the most perverted angels in the abyss, and to authorise the less guilty only, to come into our midst. His arrangement was not accepted. Preference was accorded to a ruling in virtue of which the devils of the air permutated with those of hell, in such a way that the same individual was alternatively in the abyss and in our atmosphere. This *chassé-croisé* had been glimpsed by Petrus Lombardus : it was confirmed by Suarez.

All this concerned only the demons. As for Satan, the theologians generally admitted that he had come out from hell, a first time to tempt our first parents, a second time to tempt the Saviour, but that after that he had not returned to the surface of the earth. Estius alone, preoccupied with the preservation of the traditional teaching, let the Devil come into the air to tempt mankind ; but he sent him back to his dwelling-place as soon as his mission was accomplished.[1]

Let us note that the traditional belief, expelled from theology, found refuge with the people and in the Liturgy. Without thought of the doctors and their revolutionary speculations, the faithful continued to believe that the Devil ranged about them. And the Church, which chased the Devil from the

---

[1] Melchior Cano, *In Summam*, 1, 64, 4 ; Suarez, *De angelis*, 8, 17, 2. His exposition is, on the subject of the Devil, somewhat involved. In any case, he says (10) that, since the death of Christ, the Devil has been hurled to the depths of hell and expressly forbidden to come out of it, unless it be in the days which will precede the end of the world. Estius, *In Sententias*, 2, 6, 13.

E

bodies of the possessed, which interdicted, under the gravest penalties, pacts with the Devil, changed nothing in its practices. The theologians, with their innovations, succeeded only in putting themselves in a state of rebellion against the Ritual.

CHAPTER XI

THE FATE OF THE DEVIL AND OF THE DEMONS

§ 1. THEIR PRESENT FATE

As long as the primitive regime, which placed the actual residence of the Devil and of the demons in the air, lasted, they were exempt from sensible pains during the whole duration of the present world. The texts are numerous in which the doctors tell us, or leave us to gather clearly, that the evil spirits spread throughout the atmosphere will one day suffer, but do not actually suffer now, unless through the thought of the pains which await them, which they know in advance. I will confine myself to citing the testimony of Tertullian and of Saint Augustine. This is what the first says in the *Apologeticus*, 27:

'Although the demons are subjected to us, nevertheless, like wicked slaves, they sometimes add arrogance to their fear. They are delighted to harm those whom they fear; hatred is the daughter of fear. Condemned without hope, their consolation is the evil they do while awaiting the torture reserved for them.'

As for Saint Augustine, he says (*Genesi Ad Litteram*, II, 33) :

> ' Let us not doubt but that the guilty angels were hurled into the dungeon of our shadowy atmosphere, while waiting to be punished on the Day of Judgement.'

In the middle of the twelfth century we still find Saint Bernard saying, speaking of the Devil (*Sermon*, I, 4, *On The Death of Saint Malachi*) :

> ' The Devil is not yet in the fire, but the fire is ready to receive him, and he has but little time left in which to do evil.'

Naturally, since the reform inaugurated by Petrus Lombardus, things have changed. The Devil, who, from now on, is in the depths of hell, there undergoes the torture of fire. And the demons are subjected to the same torture during the whole time they reside in hell. But when the alternation of the service arrangement calls them into the air, what is their fate? Reading Petrus Lombardus and his first disciples, one gets the impression that the sojourn in our atmosphere is a time of respite for these evil beings, during which the torture of fire is spared them. But, from the time of Albertus Magnus on, a formidable problem here arises. Let us see its occasion.

In his *Commentary upon the Epistle of St James* iii. 6, Bede compares the demons to those in a fever, who, lying in their beds, are burnt by an interior fire, and he adds that, wherever the demons betake themselves, they bear within them the fire of hell. In this author's thought, this fire is of a moral order, and he mentions the pain which their prevision of the fate which awaits them causes the fallen angels. But Albertus Magnus, reading Bede's text in the *Gloss*, in which Walafrid Strabo had inserted it, took it literally. He concluded that the demons, while they voyaged through the air and prowl all about us, are enveloped by a globe of fire which burns them. It might have been objected that, if that were so, the demons would reduce to cinders the objects near which they passed. But Albertus replied that the fire spread about the demons is at the orders of divine justice, and that its action takes effect only upon the beings whom God wishes to chastise.

It was, truly, difficult to put forth a more daring assertion than that. Saint Bonaventure dared not follow Albertus in the path he had taken, and he remained faithful to the traditional opinion, which postponed the torture of the demons until after the Last Judgement. Saint Thomas, whom more intimate ties linked to Albertus, defended the opinion of his Master in his commentary upon the *In Sententias*. Later, when he wrote his *Summa*, he made a *volte-face*. But so well did he mask his thought that he was regarded as a partisan of Albertus. Henceforth it was accepted that the demons spread throughout the atmosphere suffered from now on the torture of fire.[1]

There were, indeed, some protests. Cajetan and Melchior Cano tried to obtain appreciation for the rights of the old doctrine, that which, in the thir-

---

[1] Albertus Magnus, *In Sententias*, 2, 6, 7 ; Saint Bonaventure, *In Sententias*, 2, 6, 2, quæst, 2 ; Saint Thomas, *In Sententias*, 2, 6, 1, art., 1, 3 to 6 ; *Summa*, 1, 64, 3–4.

teenth century, Bonaventure had still defended. The
Franciscan Feuardent, who was deeply versed in the
study of Irenæus and the first Fathers, asserted that
he had come across texts where it was said that the
Devil was ignorant of his condemnation until the
coming of Christ. Feuardent was told that he had
made a mistake, and that nothing like that could be
found in ecclesiastical literature. As for Cajetan and
Melchior Cano, they were regarded as fractious persons, who distorted the sense of texts out of love
of contradiction. Doubtless, they were told, many
Fathers mentioned only the future pains of the
demons, those which these evil-doing spirits will have
to suffer after the Judgement. But they did not mean
thereby to exempt them from present pains. They
were convinced, without thinking it necessary to
explain themselves upon this point, that the guilty
angels suffer, even now, the torture of fire. And,
when they spoke of the future sufferings of the
demons, they had in view certain accessory pains
which will then be inflicted upon them for the first
time. From the Day of Judgement, in fact, the
demons will no longer be able to voyage through the
air, and they will no longer have men to draw into
evil. These are the pains which will then be inflicted
upon the infernal spirits, and which the Fathers liked
to mention, without ever speaking of the present
torture of fire. Thus, notably, spoke Suarez and
Bellarmin.[1]

[1] Cajetan, *In secundam Petri*, 2, 4 ; Feuardent, Note on Irenæus,
5, 26.   Suarez, *De angelis*, 8, 2, 3 ; Bellarmin, *De beatitudine sanctorum*,
6, 1.

Everything seemed arranged for the best. Unhappily, these complacent explanations did not obtain unanimous approval. Certain exigent minds thought that, if the Fathers had believed in the present torture of the demons who are scattered through the air, they would have said so, sometimes at least, instead of always insisting upon speaking of their future sufferings. And, respectfully, they let the theologians gather that their interpretation of the texts of the Fathers was artificial. And, to complete the misfortune, these independent minds were most erudite ones, familiarised with the Fathers by long study. They were Petau, the most learned man of his time ; and the Benedictine Mathoud, in his notes upon Robertus Pulleyn; and finally Huet, author of the *Origeniana*. A protest signed by men so imposing was such as to call for reflection. And, in fact, they found some adherents. But the scholastics did not read Petau, nor Mathoud, nor Huet, and they brought the texts of the Fathers to the decisions of Albertus Magnus and Saint Thomas.[1]

It did not suffice to assert that the demons suffered in the air the torture of fire; it still had to be explained how they suffered it ; and this task was difficult. Albertus Magnus, as we have said, imagined that the demons drew after them, wherever they went, a globe of fire, which enveloped them and tortured them, but

---

[1] Petau, *De angelis*, 3, 4, 19 ; Mathoud, notes on Robertus Pulleyn, 2, 5, in Migne 186, 1027 ; Huet, *Origeniana*, 2, 2, 5, 23. Huet only touches on the question, but it can be seen that he places himself beside Petau. Bellarmin was held to have said the last word on the question. See Estius, *In Sententias*, 2, 6, 14 ; Tournely, *De angelis*, 11, 1 object, 2.

which, by a divine dispensation, was at once inoffensive and invisible to our eyes. Saint Thomas did not accept this explanation. In his commentary upon the *In Sententias* he taught that the fire which burns the demons in the air is not in immediate contact with them, that it remains confined to hell, and that it tortures these victims at a distance. Ripened by experience and study, the angelic doctor doubtless found, later, that the hypothesis of action at a distance was not very satisfactory. In the *Summa*, in fact, after having asserted that the demons spread throughout the air are subjected from now on to the sensible pains of hell, he explains their torture in the following way :

> ' The demons who dwell in the air are not, it is true, actually bound by the fire of Gehenna ; but they know that one day they will be united to this fire, and that is why they suffer now what they will suffer hereafter.'

Albertus' theory, which Saint Thomas himself had rejected, found few partisans. Suarez reproached him with making too great a use of miracles. How could one admit, in fact, that globes of fire surround us without their presence manifesting itself to us ? Doubtless God is all-powerful, and can do everything He wishes. But He does not multiply miracles without need. Now, in Albertus' system, the laws of nature would be perpetually violated. By these objections Suarez gave its death-blow to a doctrine which, in any case, had until then only vegetated. And henceforward there was no further question of making the demons voyage in globes of fire.

The same doctor deals faithfully with the explanation to be read in the *Summa*. We have seen that, in his second view, Saint Thomas did not submit the demons actually to the reach of the fire. With what right then did he set himself against those who, according to his own words, ' postponed to the Day of Judgement the sensible pain of the fire ? ' Doubtless, he set in relief the prevision that the demons have of their fate, and he presented this prevision as a source of suffering to them. But who then had refused to the rebel angels the anticipated knowledge of the tortures which await them ? Who, then, had denied that this knowledge makes them unhappy ? No one, surely. On the contrary, the Fathers often showed Satan's companions as miserable beings. Only, they did not confuse the prevision of the torture with the torture itself. They knew that, in spite of all subtleties, between the apprehension and the torture itself there is always the distance that separates a moral from a physical pain. Thus between the formulæ of the *Summa* and those of the Fathers the only perceptible difference was that between a doctrine which displays itself openly and a doctrine which hides itself beneath a different label. Suarez saw this fault and illuminated it. He reproached the angelic doctor with upholding a theory of which he was declaring himself an adversary, and of sustaining with one hand what he was overthrowing with the other.[1]

After vigorously combating the explanation of the

[1] Saint Thomas, *Summa*, 1, 64, 3–4. Estius, 2, 6, 14 (end), points out in this text of the *Summa*, compared with the commentary on the *In Sententias*, an unavowed evolution ; Suarez, 8, 7, 35 ; 8, 14, 16 ; and 9, 16, 35.

Summa, Suarez fell back upon that which the angelic
doctor had presented in his *Commentary upon the
Sentences,* and he made himself its defender. Unhappily it, too, was not free from one objection. For it
was not natural, in very truth, that fire should exert
its action from the depths of hell upon creatures
scattered throughout the air. And if the invisible fire
of Albertus multiplied miracles beyond measure, the
same reproach could be made to Suarez' fire which,
without coming forth from hell, hurled metaphysical
entities at spirits moving about at our sides, without
ever attacking us. Thus, in spite of the blows which
the great Spanish doctor had given it, the explanation
of the *Summa* kept its partisans. In order to make
it acceptable, it sufficed to meet with silence the
objections it called forth, and to reserve criticisms for
the action of fire at a distance. Thus did Estius.[1]

§ 2. THE FUTURE FATE OF THE DEVIL AND THE DEMONS

Origen, for whom punishment had a medicinal
character, thought that all men, even the most guilty,
would be converted after punishment proportional
to their faults, and would, in the end, enter heaven.
His ideas about the future fate of the demons are
expressed in the following passage from his book,
De Principiis, 1, 6, 3 :

' Some of those who work under the orders of
the Devil and who adhere to his perversity—can
these, in future centuries, return to the good, in

[1] Suarez, 6, 16, 36 ; Estius, 2, 6, 14.

virtue of the free choice that is in them? . . . It is for you, reader to decide. . . . In any case, these beings are classed according to their merits . . . some earlier, others later, at the end of long and rigorous tortures, will first come back into the ranks of the angels, then they will raise themselves to superior degrees, and they will attain to the invisible and eternal regions, after filling, as a trial, the diverse heavenly ministries.'

So much for the demons. Now for the Devil (*De Principiis*, 3, 6, 5):

' The last enemy, which we call death, will be destroyed, so that there will be no more sadness, death being ended, and no more opposition, the enemy being gone. This last enemy will be destroyed, not in the sense that his substance, made by God, will be annihilated, but in the sense that the perversity of his will, which is his own work, and not the work of God, will disappear.'

Huet, Bishop of Avranches, perceives that, in this slightly enigmatic text, death means the Devil. Thus Origen believes in the definitive salvation of the diabolic army, its chief, Satan, included.

Origen had, in the East, numerous disciples, among whom I will confine myself to mentioning here Saint Gregory of Nyssa. Among the doctors of the West he numbers one notable disciple, that is, Saint Jerome. In his *Catechetical Lectures*, 26, 5 and 9, Gregory of Nyssa says that God, when He accomplished the mystery of the Incarnation, did well

' not only to the lost creature (man), but even to

the author of our fall . . . he delivered man from sin and healed the very author of sin.'

Gregory believes that the Devil is, even now, converted.

Jerome who, after 394, was Origen's most determined adversary, began by being his passionate admirer. In the second period of his life he limited himself to teaching that all Christians would be saved, and he refused salvation to the Devil. The following text from the *Commentary upon the Epistle to the Ephesians* iv. 6, written about 390, tells us what he thought in his first period :

' At the time of the universal restoration, when the true physician, Jesus the Christ, will come to heal the body of the Church, that to-day is divided and torn, each . . . will again take up his rank and become what he was in the beginning . . . the apostate will find once more his primitive condition, and man will return to the paradise whence he was cast out.' [1]

The unknown writer whom we call the *Ambrosiaster*, and who, about 390, wrote at Rome a *Commentary upon the Epistles of St Paul*, promised salvation not only to all the Christians, but to the demons themselves.[2] But this liberal opinion, upon

[1] Later, when this troublesome text was set before him by Rufinus, Jerome got out of the difficulty by pure audacity : he pretended that, in this passage, he had confined himself to the functions of a reporter, and had in no way spoken in his own name (*Apologia adversus libros Rufini*, 1, 27). The honest Tillemont (12, 115) does not conceal the uneasiness that this charlatan scapeway causes him.

[2] *In Ephes.*, 3, 10. The author declares that the ministry of the Church aids the demons to detach themselves from the Devil.

which Saint Jerome himself waged, during the last twenty-five years of his life, violent war, did not take root in the Church. From the fifth century onwards, the Devil and the demons were inexorably condemned to sojourn in hell, at least after the end of the world.

§ 3. THE TORTURE OF THE DEVIL
AND THE DEMONS

We touch here upon a profound mystery, that Saint Thomas did not succeed in solving, which, even, caused him some loss of prestige. This is what is in question :

Before the reform introduced into Latin theology by Hugo St Victor, the fate of the diabolic army in hell raised no difficulty. Air coming in contact with fire is heated and becomes burning. The demons and their chief possessed aerial bodies. Wherefore, subjected to the fire of hell, they necessarily suffered frightful agonies. But, on the day when the demons became pure spirit-beings, free from any material element, the situation changed. Heat is a substance of material order, with which a spiritual substance can have nothing in common, and there would be as much impertinence in wanting to heat a spirit as in trying to hear a smell or paint a sound. Henceforward, how can the Devil and the demons suffer from the fire of hell ? Here is the reply that Saint Thomas gave to this question in the *Summa contra Gentiles*, 4, 90 (an answer identical in substance with that in the *Commentary upon the Sentences*, 4, 44, 3, 3, and which is reproduced in the supplement to the *Summa theologica*, 70, 3) :

'We must not imagine that incorporeal substances can undergo the action of material fire in the sense that fire can corrupt their nature, alter it or produce in it any change similar to that which it produces in our corruptible bodies. Incorporeal substances have not the corporeal nature which is requisite to undergo the action modifying corporeal things. Neither can they receive sensible forms, unless it be in the form of ideas. . . . It is thus in its quality of tie that corporeal fire can make incorporeal substances suffer. For indeed, spirits can be tied to bodies, either as forms, as, for instance, the soul is tied to the human body to give it life, or in some other way, as, for instance, necromancers do, who, by the aid of demons, attach spirits to images or to analogous objects. Therefore, the divine power can, all the more, tie the spirits of the damned to corporeal fire. Now to know themselves tied, as a means of punishment, to base things, is for them a source of affliction.'

In the *Commentary upon the Sentences*, we read this additional explanation :

' The spirit is in a state of detention in the fire, a state which has a penal character, because the fire prevents the spirit from accomplishing its will and from doing what it wishes.'

This explanation of the torture of the demons in hell was already to be found in Albertus Magnus

(4, 44, 37). Saint Thomas, therefore, is not its author. He received it from his masters and confined himself to giving it the support of his name. This support was efficacious. For nearly three centuries the Schoolmen, with very few exceptions, taught that the torment of the demons consisted in being in a state of detention in the fire of hell. But a day came when the insufficiency of this theory was made plain. The opposition, begun by the Dominican Soto, was fed, above all, by the Jesuits. We read in Lessius (*De perfectionibus divinis*, 13, 215) :

'If it were a question only of imprisoning the demons, blocks of stone or mounds of earth would fulfil this rôle much better than fire, which is very light and has no density. Wherefore, then, did Our Lord say that fire was prepared for the Devil and his angels from the beginning ? Besides, if the demons do not undergo in the fire any other pain than that of imprisonment, this is also the only pain from which the souls of the damned now suffer who (until the Resurrection) are simply spirits. Now the soul of the bad rich man of the Gospel does not ask for liberation, it says that it is tortured in the fire. Which shows us that the souls of the damned are suffering now in hell that which they will suffer later when they will have their bodies. Besides, such is the opinion of the faithful.'

This last argument was very strong. If the fire of hell confines itself to imprisoning the demons, it has no other action upon the souls of the damned from now until the Resurrection, and we must say that the

latter are simply imprisoned in hell. Now such is not
the opinion of the faithful, and the theory of Saint
Thomas, which was adopted by all the greatest
Schoolmen, conflicted with the popular belief.

It broke itself upon it. Nearly all the theologians,
from the sixteenth century onwards, taught that the
fire of hell is not only a place of detention for the
demons and the damned souls until the Resurrection,
but is also a source of physical pain. Only a few
ardent Thomists stood out. And one of them,
Billuart (*De angelis*, 6, 3) consented to recognise that
the popular belief was not absurd. He maintained
only that imprisonment is the one torture mentioned
by Saint Thomas, and that the rest is uncertain.[1]

Thus the Devil and the demons are physically
tortured by the fire of hell. How? Suarez (*De
angelis*, 8, 14, 41) explained that the aforesaid fire
sent to the demons a pain-bearing spiritual quality,
whose result was spiritual pain. It might have been
objected that a body is totally incapable of producing a spiritual quality; that a pain produced
by a spiritual quality can have nothing in common
with a sensation of heat; and that any other body
might have produced the pain sent by the fire to
the demons.

But Suarez settled the objection in advance (45),
by observing that the pain-bearing spiritual quality
surpassed the range of our minds. In reality, the pain-
bearing spiritual quality imagined by Suarez was

---

[1] According to Billuart, who is here the authentic interpreter of
Saint Thomas, the pain of the demons comes from the fact that they
are enchained by an object which, for them, is ' most vile '—*rei
vilissimæ*. This pain is thus the feeling of humiliation.

[Photo : Grillot de Givry

SATAN ON HIS THRONE

[Photo : Rieder

THE MAW OF HELL, AS IT WAS REPRESENTED
IN THE MEDIÆVAL THEATRE
(The origin of the Harlequinade)

simply the old doctrine of imprisonment, dressed out under a new name.

Petau began by declaring (*De angelis*, 3, 5, 11), that it is as impossible to heat a spirit as it is to coat it with a layer of paint, and he mocked the theologians who surpassed themselves in explaining the inexplicable. He added that, according to nearly all the Schoolmen, the pain felt by the demons comes from the imprisonment to which they are condemned. He concludes (13):

> 'For our own part, we think that, as well as the pain of imprisonment, the fire inflicts upon the demons another unknown pain; otherwise its intervention would have no reason, and it would do nothing more than does the earth, which circumscribes hell. . . . Thus I believe that the demons and the souls of the damned are burnt by the fire, but I do not know how.'

It is this solution which was adopted in the course of the last century. It is not known how the demons (and the damned, from now to the Resurrection) are burnt in hell; but it is felt certain that they are. Saint Thomas and all the great Schoolmen who walked with him are abandoned. Strictly, we ought to return to him, now that Thomism is the official doctrine of the Church. Are we going to obey logic? Miscreants who may be inclined to take no interest in the question should note this: as heretics they are destined to hell. Now the ruling in force to-day permits the fire of hell to inflict upon them frightful torments immediately after their death, while, ac-

F

cording to the legislation of Saint Thomas, this same fire would confine itself, until the resurrection of the body, to a mere prison wall. It offers them all the more appreciable an advantage inasmuch as the Resurrection may, peradventure, be long in coming. They should, therefore, desire a return to the Thomist tradition. I warn them, though, that their desire will not be realised. The popular belief, which expelled from theology the theory of the great Schoolmen, will be well able to prevent its return. It has won far more difficult victories over the doctors, notably on the subject of the Immaculate Conception. Its triumph here is not in doubt. And the dictatorship exercised by Saint Thomas must not delude us ; it stops short before the faith of the faithful.

PART THREE

The Activities of the Devil on Earth before the Foundation of the Church

CHAPTER XII

VICTIMS OF THE DEVIL BEFORE THE COMING OF CHRIST

AFTER he had slaked his rage in Heaven, the Devil turned to earth to overwhelm it with evils. The victims of his perversity were innumerable. I shall speak of some of those who lived before the coming of Christ.

§ I. ADAM AND EVE

The first of all were Adam and Eve. They were happy. They dwelt in a garden of delight, well-watered and bounteous. All the fruits of the trees were at their choice, save only the fruits of the tree of the knowledge of good and evil. Those they might not touch, under pain of death. Let *Genesis* iii. tell the story:

'Now the serpent was more subtil than any beast of the field which the Lord God had made. And he said unto the woman, Yea, hath God said, Ye shall not eat of any tree of the garden? And the woman said unto the serpent, Of the fruit of the trees of the garden we may eat: but of the fruit of the tree which is in the midst of the garden,

God hath said, Ye shall not eat of it, lest ye die.
And the serpent said unto the woman, Ye shall not
surely die : for God doth know that, in the day ye
eat thereof, then your eyes shall be opened, and ye
shall be as gods, knowing good and evil.

'And when the woman saw that the tree was
good for food, and that it was a delight to the eyes,
and that the tree was to be desired to make one
wise, she took of the fruit thereof, and did eat :
and she gave also unto her husband with her, and
he did eat. And the eyes of them both were opened,
and they knew that they were naked : and they
sewed fig leaves together, and made themselves
aprons. And they heard the voice of the Lord God,
walking in the garden in the cool of the day : and
the man and his wife hid themselves from the
presence of the Lord God amongst the trees of the
garden.

'And the Lord God called unto the man and
said unto him, Where art thou ? And he said, I
heard thy voice in the garden, and I was afraid,
because I was naked ; and I hid myself. And he
said, Who told thee that thou wast naked ? Hast
thou eaten of the tree, whereof I commanded thee,
that thou shouldest not eat ? And the man said,
The woman whom thou gavest to be with me, she
gave me of the tree, and I did eat. And the Lord
God said unto the woman, What is this that thou
hast done ? And the woman said, The serpent
beguiled me, and I did eat. And the Lord said unto
the serpent, Because thou hast done this, cursed
art thou above all cattle, and above every beast of

the field ; upon thy belly shalt thou go, and dust shalt thou eat all the days of thy life : and I will put enmity between thee and the woman, and between thy seed and her seed : it shall bruise thy head, and thou shalt bruise his heel. Unto the woman he said, I will greatly multiply thy sorrow and thy conception : in sorrow shalt thou bring forth children : and thy desire shall be to thy husband, and he shall rule over thee. And unto Adam he said, Because thou hast hearkened unto the voice of thy wife, and hast eaten of the fruit, of which I commanded thee, saying, Thou shalt not eat of it ; in toil shalt thou eat of it all the days of thy life : thorns also and thistles shall it bring forth to thee ; and thou shalt eat the herb of the field ; in the sweat of thy face shalt thou eat bread, till thou return unto the ground, for out of it wast thou taken : for dust thou art, and unto dust shalt thou return.'

In this account there are two things to distinguish : the text and the interpretation that the Fathers have given to the text.

The text shows us the serpent in conversation with Eve, and the dialogue that passes between these two recalls to memory this observation of Bossuet's (*Elévations sur les Mystères*, 6, 1) :

' A serpent speaks : a woman listens : a man, so perfect and greatly enlightened, lets himself be drawn into a gross temptation : the whole human race falls with him into sin and into death : *all this seems senseless.*'

But the Fathers, beginning with Saint Justin, teach us that the serpent was, in that instance, the instrument of an invisible being, and that our first mother conversed, in reality, not with the serpent, but with the spirit for whom the serpent served as an envelope. Nothing in the text of *Genesis* permits us to glimpse or even to suspect the presence of a spirit.[1] The historian Josephus who, at the beginning of his *Jewish Antiquities* relates the origin of the human race, reproduces the Biblical account without adding to it. And the passage in *Wisdom*, ii. 24-25, where we read that death was brought to earth by the jealousy of the Devil, is a Christian interpolation wholly foreign to the text.[2] Thus the interpretation favoured by the Fathers is their own work, or, more exactly, the work of the earliest of them, Saint Justin, who uses it in his *Dialogue*, 103, 5; 112, 5. It was the period when Marcion was blaspheming the Creator, whom he made responsible for the ills of the human race. To which Justin replied that the present misery of the human race has for responsible author an erring angel, and not God, who did not desire it. In a word, since Justin, the Devil has been the cause of the downfall of the human race.

[1] In *Numbers* xxii. 28, Balaam's ass speaks to her master, who sees nothing strange in her speaking. The interpretation accepted by the Fathers is artificial, and depends upon a complete misunderstanding of the minds of primitive people.

[2] The original edition of *Wisdom* went straight on from ii. 22 to iii. 1: "The impious understand nought of the reward of pure souls (they understand nought because they are ignorant of the life to come). The souls of the righteous are in the hand of God." In the description of the righteous in chapter ii. v. 13, and verses 17–20 are Christian interpolations.

§ 2. OTHER VICTIMS

We must here mention three other victims of the Devil before the coming of Christ.

The first is King Saul, of whose misfortunes the Bible tells us in these words (1 *Samuel* xvi. 14-23):

' Now the spirit of the Lord had departed from Saul, and an evil spirit from the Lord troubled him. And Saul's servants said unto him, Behold now, an evil spirit from God troubleth thee. Let our lord now command thy servants, which are before thee, to seek out a man who is a cunning player on the harp ; and it shall come to pass, when the evil spirit from God is upon thee, that he shall play with his hand, and thou shalt be well . . . (the choice of the servants falls upon David). . . . And it came to pass, when the evil spirit from God was upon Saul, that David took the harp, and played with his hand : so Saul was refreshed and was well, and the evil spirit departed from him . . . (xviii. 10). And it came to pass on the morrow that an evil spirit from God came mightily upon Saul, and he raved in the midst of the house.'

Our texts do not hesitate to say that the ' evil spirit' which tormented Saul came ' from the Lord', and that it was the evil spirit of God. But, in the commentaries of the Fathers and the theologians, this evil spirit becomes a subaltern of Satan.

The second victim is the holy man, Job, con-

cerning whom the Bible gives the following information (*Job* i. 6) :

'Now there was a day when the sons of God
came to present themselves before the Lord, and
Satan came also among them. And the Lord said
unto Satan, Whence comest thou? Then Satan
answered the Lord, and said, From going to and
fro in the earth, and from walking up and down in
it. And the Lord said unto Satan, Hast thou considered my servant Job? for there is none like
him in the earth, a perfect and an upright man, one
that feareth God, and escheweth evil. Then Satan
answered the Lord, and said, Doth Job fear God
for nought? Hast not thou made an hedge about
his house, and about all that he hath, on every side?
thou hast blessed the work of his hands, and his
substance is increased in the land. But put forth
thine hand now, and touch all that he hath, and he
will renounce thee to thy face. And the Lord said
unto Satan, Behold, all that he hath is in thy power;
only upon himself put not forth thine hand. . . .
(Job loses all his riches and his children at one fell
swoop, but remains, nevertheless, faithful to the
Lord.)

'ii. 1. Again there was a day when the sons of God
came to present themselves before the Lord, and
Satan came also among them to present himself
before the Lord. And the Lord said unto Satan,
Whence comest thou? And Satan answered the
Lord, and said, From going to and fro in the earth,
and from walking up and down in it. And the Lord

said unto Satan, Hast thou considered my servant Job? for there is none like him in the earth, a perfect and an upright man, one that feareth God and escheweth evil; and he still holdest fast his integrity, although thou movedst me against him to destroy him without cause. And Satan answered the Lord, and said, Skin for skin, yea, all that a man hath will he give for his life. But put forth thine hand now and touch his bone and his flesh, and he will renounce thee to thy face. And the Lord said unto Satan, Behold, he is in thine hand; only spare his life. So Satan went forth from the presence of the Lord, and smote Job with sore boils from the sole of his foot unto his crown.' (Job remains faithful to the Lord.)

Here Satan is one of God's officials, put in charge of the Ministry of Police by his master. He ranges over the earth to carry out his inspections. When his inquiry is completed, he goes to the heavenly court to draw up his report. He offers suggestions to God, who approves them. He says to his master: ' Job's virtue, which you admire so much, is not disinterested. Let me strike him and you will see this façade crumble !' When he has received powers, he exercises them, but without ever overstepping them. He strikes Job only up to the point which God has authorised. He is a conscientious servant. Writing four centuries before the Christian era, the author of the *Book of Job* did not possess the light upon Satan which the Fathers and the theologians were to acquire later, and the personage whose portrait he draws is far from the Christian Devil. But the Fathers and theologians have identified him with the rebel archangel : it is because of this that he has his place here.

The third victim is the young Sarah, daughter of Raguel of Ecbatana (*Rages* in the Vulgate), whose trial is described in these terms in the Bible (*Tobit* iii. 8) :

> ' She had been married to seven husbands, whom Asmodeus the evil spirit had killed before they had lain with her. Dost thou not know, said they, that thou has strangled thine husbands ? '

The heart-broken maiden with tears entreated God to take pity on her. The angel Raphael gave to the young Tobias a recipe : he was to roast the heart and liver of a fish. Before joining himself to Sarah, Tobias carried out the angelic instructions. Then (viii. 2— Greek) :

> ' The demon, as soon as he smelt the smell, fled into Upper Egypt, where the angel (Raphael) bound him.'

The demon Asmodeus has for cradle the book of the Avesta, where he is called *Aêshma*. The Persians completed this name by adding to it the word *daêva* (God), and they called the genie of concupiscence *Aêshma-daêva*. Asmodeus is thus of Persian origin. Naturally, when he penetrated into Christian theology, he accepted the nature imposed by the Fathers upon the bad angels, and he became a satellite of Satan.

The Old Testament furnishes us with two other

pieces of information about the Devil. The first is in the following text of *Zechariah* iii. 1 :

'And he shewed me Joshua the high priest standing before the angel of the Lord, and Satan standing at his right hand to be his adversary. And the (angel of the) Lord said unto Satan, The Lord rebuke thee, O Satan ! yea, the Lord that hath chosen Jerusalem rebuke thee ! '

The second comes from 1 *Chronicles* xxi. 1, where we read :

' And Satan stood up against Israel, and moved David to number Israel. And David said to Joab, and to the princes of the people : Go, number Israel. . . . And God was displeased with this thing ; therefore he smote Israel. . . . So the Lord sent a pestilence upon Israel ; and there fell of Israel seventy thousand men. And God sent an angel to Jerusalem to destroy it ; and as he was about to destroy, the Lord beheld, and he repented him of the evil.'

In the text of *Zechariah* (later than the Captivity) as in *Job*, Satan has his *entrée* to the heavenly court. He makes an unfavourable report upon the high priest Joshua as upon Joshua's predecessors. His objective is evidently to obtain from God orders which shall be harmful either to Joshua or to the priesthood in general. But his requisition is refused. As in the *Book of Job*, Satan is a prefect of police. Preoccupied with the maintenance of order, he treats mankind without mercy, and asks sanctions of God.

His suggestions which, in the *Book of Job*, were adopted, are not adopted here : his report is not followed up by any sanction.

The text of *Chronicles* is the corrected version of a passage from 2 *Samuel* xxiv. 1, where we read :

> 'And again the anger of the Lord was kindled against Israel, and he moved David against them, saying, Go, number Israel and Judah. And the king said to Joab ... Go now to and fro through all the tribes of Israel . . . and number ye the people. . . . So the Lord sent a pestilence upon Israel, from the morning even to the time appointed : and there died of the people from Dan even to Beer-sheba seventy thousand men. . . .'

The two accounts tell us of a numbering which provokes the chastisement of God. Only, according to 2 *Samuel*, it is God Himself who, in anger, suggests this numbering to David, in order to have a pretext for chastising Israel. In *Chronicles*, Satan is substituted for God, and he becomes the author of the offending census. This substitution is evidently inspired by a desire to protect God's honour in a particular case where this honour was compromised. It has no other reason. The Satan of *Chronicles* who takes the responsibility for an odious measure remains the prefect of police that he is in the *Book of Job* and in *Zechariah* ; and the fit of wickedness which animates him is transitory. We must recognise, however, that he accomplishes the evil before receiving from God instructions to do it. Without being the Christian Devil, he is his precursor.

A word in conclusion upon the following verse from *Ecclesiasticus* xxi. 27 (21, 30 of the Vulgate) :

'When the ungodly curseth Satan he curseth his own soul.'

This laconic text is an indecipherable enigma. Not knowing what the author meant, we are quite unable to define his conception of Satan. If he means an angelic spirit, there is nothing to prevent his thinking of this spirit as the policeman of the *Book of Job* and of *Zechariah.*

CHAPTER XIII

THE DEVIL PERSECUTES THE
CONTEMPORARIES OF CHRIST

THE Devil who, since Adam's sin, had intervened but rarely in the affairs of mankind,
abandoned his reserve upon the approach of the
Christian era and, by himself or through his subordinates, inflicted manifold evils upon mankind.
Truth to tell, the popular legends of all lands had long
told of this horrid activity. But they had not penetrated cultivated circles. We have to await the theologians of Persia and the school of Pythagoras to see
the learned paying attention to the beliefs of the
people. The *Book of Enoch*, which has taken advantage of the teachings of the school of Pythagoras,
tells us (15) that the beings procreated by the lustful
angels are :

'Evil spirits upon the earth, and on the earth
shall be their dwelling.'

Such was the situation when Christ descended
from heaven into Palestine. The following texts
tell us of the spectacle which Jesus had before His
eyes :

St Mark i. 23 : 'And straightway there was in
their synagogue a man with an unclean spirit ; and

he cried out saying, What have we to do with thee, thou Jesus of Nazareth? art thou come to destroy us?'

St Mark v. 2: 'And when he was come out of the boat, straightway there met him out of the tombs a man with an unclean spirit, who had his dwelling in the tombs; and no man could any more bind him, no, not with a chain; because that he had been often bound with fetters and chains, and the chains had been rent asunder by him, and the fetters broken in pieces; and no man had strength to tame him. And always, night and day, in the tombs and in the mountains, he was crying out and cutting himself with stones. And when he saw Jesus from afar, he ran and worshipped him; and crying out with a loud voice, he saith, What have I to do with thee, Jesus, thou Son of the Most High God?'

St Mark vii. 25: 'But straightway a woman, whose little daughter had an unclean spirit, having heard of him, came and fell down at his feet. Now the woman was a Greek, a Syrophœnician by race.'

St Mark ix. 17: 'And one of the multitude answered him, Master, I brought unto thee my son, which hath a dumb spirit; and wheresoever it taketh him, it dasheth him down; and he foameth, and grindeth his teeth, and pineth away.'

St Luke viii. 2: . . . (in the company of Jesus were) 'certain women, which had been healed of evil spirits and infirmities, Mary that was called

G

Magdalene, from whom seven demons had gone out. . . .'

St Luke xiii. 11 : 'And behold, a woman which had a spirit of infirmity eighteen years ; and she was bowed together, and could in nowise lift herself up.'

Chapter XIV

THE DEVIL ATTACKS CHRIST HIMSELF

SATAN had been the master of the human race since the day when he had induced Adam to sin. After several thousand years, Christ had pity upon mankind, and He came upon earth to tear them from the hands of their gaoler. The letters of Ignatius of Antioch (*Ephesians* xix. 1) inform us that He hid His coming from the Devil.[1] But the latter had, nevertheless, a suspicion, whose result was the scene of the Temptation. This is what we read on this subject in *Luke* iv. 3 :

'And the Devil said unto him, If thou art the Son of God, command this stone, that it become bread. And Jesus answered unto him, It is written, Man shall not live by bread alone.

'And he led him up and shewed him all the kingdoms of the world in a moment of time. And the Devil said unto him, To thee will I give all this authority, and the glory of them ; for it hath been delivered unto me ; and to whomsoever I will, I give it. If thou therefore wilt worship before me, it shall all be thine. And Jesus answered and said unto him, It is written, Thou shalt

[1] Delafosse, *Lettres d'Ignace d'Antioche*, p. 103.

worship the Lord thy God, and him only shalt thou serve.

'And he led him to Jerusalem, and set him on the pinnacle of the temple, and said unto him, If thou art the Son of God, cast thyself down from hence; for it is written, He shall give his angels charge over thee, to guard thee, and on their hands they shall bear thee up, lest haply thou dash thy foot against a stone. And Jesus answering said unto him, It is said, Thou shalt not tempt the Lord thy God.'

The Temptation was the first attack of the Devil upon Christ: an attack which proved fruitless. Undiscouraged, Satan determined to encompass the death of the Saviour. For it is upon him that the responsibility falls for the drama of Calvary, as the following text from *St Luke* xxii. 3 shows:

'And Satan entered into Judas who was called Iscariot, being of the number of the twelve. And he went away and communed with the chief priests and captains, how he might deliver him unto them.'

And similarly *St John*, after mentioning the sop given by Jesus to Judas in the course of the Last Supper says (xiii. 27):

'And after the sop, then entered Satan into him. Jesus therefore saith unto him, That thou doest, do quickly.'

Thus it is indeed the Devil who, by the intermediary of Judas, delivered up Christ to the Romans.

It is he who crucified the Saviour. To this Jesus'
words to Pilate allude (*St John* xix. 11) :

> ' Jesus answered him, Thou wouldest have no
> power against me, except it were given thee from
> above ; therefore he that delivered me unto thee
> hath greater sin.' [1]

[1] The intervention of Satan in the death of Christ is foreign to the
primitive tradition. The text of *Luke* xxii. 3 belongs to a later version.
The same observation applies to *Luke* xiii. 16, where Satan is mentioned.
As for the text of *John*, see Delafosse, *Le Quatrième Evangile*, p. 19.

CHAPTER XV

CHRIST CASTS OUT THE DEMONS AND OVERTHROWS THE DOMINION OF THE DEVIL UPON EARTH

THE texts cited above have shown us that, at the time of Christ, the demons—that is to say, the subordinates of Satan—often chose to reside in the bodies of men. The following texts will show that Christ, when occasion arose, often dislodged them from their resorts :

St Mark i. 25 : ' And Jesus rebuked (the unclean spirit) saying, Hold thy peace, and come out of him. And the unclean spirit, tearing him and crying with a loud voice, came out of him. And they were all amazed, insomuch that they questioned among themselves, saying, What is this ? A new teaching ! with authority he commandeth even the unclean spirits and they obey him.'

St Mark v. 7 : ' (The unclean spirit saith to Jesus), I adjure thee by God, torment me not. For he said unto him, Come forth, thou unclean spirit, out of the man. And he asked him, What is thy name ? And he saith unto him, My name is Legion ; for we are many. And he besought him much, that he would not send him away out of the country. Now there was there on the mountainside a great herd of swine feeding. And they besought him, saying, Send us into the swine, that we may enter into them. And he gave them leave. And the unclean spirits came out, and entered into the swine; and the herd rushed down the steep into the sea, in number about two thousand; and they were choked in the sea. And they that fed them fled, and told it in the city and in the country. And they came to see what it was that had come to pass. And they came to Jesus, and beheld him that was possessed with devils sitting, clothed and in his right mind, even him that had the legion; and they were afraid.'

St Mark ix. 25 : 'And when Jesus saw that a multitude came running together, he rebuked the unclean spirit, saying unto him, Thou dumb and deaf spirit, I command thee, come out of him, and enter no more into him. And having cried out, and torn him much, he came out; and the child became as one dead; insomuch that the more part said, He is dead. But Jesus took him by the hand, and raised him up; and he arose.'

Further, Jesus cured the daughter of the Greek woman and the woman bowed down for eighteen years.

The lieutenants of Satan were, on many occasions, expelled by Christ. But Satan himself gained a brilliant victory over Christ, since he succeeded in crucifying Him. But never was victory more ephemeral! Satan had scarce ended his toil when he suffered a double defeat : a defeat upon earth, where mankind was delivered from his yoke, a defeat in hell, which ceased to be under his dominion. The victor was vanquished.

Here let us consider the defeat of Satan upon earth.

The exegesists think that this defeat of the Devil was foretold by Christ Himself in the following text from *St Luke* x. 17 :

'I beheld Satan fallen as lightning from heaven.'

But here Satan means the Roman Empire. It is the approaching fall of the power of Rome which is predicted in this prophecy, and not that of the Devil. But the ruin of the latter is foretold by Jesus in this text from *St John* xii. 31 :

'Now shall the prince of this world be cast out.'

The Fathers, since Saint Irenæus, are inexhaustible upon the subject of the dissolution which the death of Christ produced in the kingdom of the Devil. Since we cannot here give all their testimony, we will give some texts from Saint Augustine and from Saint Gregory the Great, who are the greatest doctors of the Church.[1]

Here is what we read in Saint Augustine :

Sermon 130, 2 : 'To be born, to labour, and to die. . . . This is the merchandise of our country : these things here abound. To such merchandise did that Merchant descend. And forasmuch as every merchant gives and receives ; gives what he

[1] See the studies of Gallerand on the Redemption in the *Revue d'Histoire et de Littérature religieuse*, 1922, and in the *Revue de l'Histoire des religions*, 1925.

has and receives what he has not . . . so Christ, too, in this His traffic, gave and received. . . . The Lord has both created and redeemed His servants ; created them that they might be ; redeemed them, that they might not be captives ever. For we fell into the hands of the prince of this world, who seduced Adam, and made him his servant, and began to possess us as his slaves. But the Redeemer came, and the seducer was overcome. And what did our Redeemer to him who held us captive ? For our ransom, He held out *His Cross as a trap :* He placed *as a bait* His Blood. He indeed had power to shed His Blood, he did not attain to drink It. And in that he shed the Blood of Him Who was no debtor, he was commanded to render up the debtors. He verily shed His Blood to this end, that He might wipe out our sins. That, then, whereby he held us fast, was effaced by the Redeemer's Blood.'

Sermon 134, 4-6: ' Come, Lord, Redeemer come, come ; Let the captive acknowledge Thee, him that leadeth captive flee Thee. . . . The Blood of the Redeemer was shed, and the debtors' bond was cancelled. . . . What meaneth this, then, thy senseless exultation, O thou that didst hold me captive, for that my Deliverer had mortal Flesh ? . . . If thou hadst found anything of thine in Him, hold Him fast . . . He did not therefore not find Flesh, but nothing of his own, that is, no sin. *Thou didst slay the Innocent :* thou destroyedst Him from Whom thou hadst nothing due, *render back what thou didst hold fast.* Why then didst thou exult for a short hour, because thou didst find in Christ mortal Flesh? *It was thy trap:* whereupon thou didst rejoice, thereby hast thou been taken.'

Sermon 263, 1-2: ' The Devil exulted when Christ was dead, and by that very death he was vanquished. He took *a bait as in a trap.* He exulted in death . . . that which rejoiced him was a trap for him. The Cross of the Lord was *a trap for the devil.* The death of the Lord was the bait by which he was to be taken.'

De Trinitate 13, 15-27 : ' It is by a certain justice of God that human kind has been delivered into the power of the Devil, since the sin of the first man passes originally into all those born by the union of the sexes. . . . But the Devil must have been vanquished by justice and not by the power of God. . . . How was he vanquished? Because he killed Christ, when he had found in Him nothing which merited death. Truly, it is just that the debtors should be set at liberty by Him who held in His power all who believe in Him. He killed, without finding in Him any debt. . . . This is why it is said that we are justified by the blood of Christ . . . Christ goes to His Passion in order to pay for us debtors a debt which He did not owe. Would the Devil have been vanquished by *this very perfect right* if Christ had wished to act through him with power and not with justice? But he relegated to the second place what he could, in order to do first what should be done. . . .The

Devil was vanquished when he believed himself to be the victor, that is to say, when Christ was killed. . . . So that those whom the Devil held justly must justly be released by him, because of Him, upon Whom he had inflicted the pain of death unjustly, since He was guilty of no sin. It was by this justice that he was vanquished. In this redemption the blood of Christ was given as a price, *but this price received by the Devil* did not enrich him, but bound him. . . . The Devil held our sins, and through them he righteously dragged us into death. These sins were cast out by He Who had no sins and Who was unjustly led to death by the Devil.'

De libero arbitrio, 3, 29-31: 'God decided, in the spirit of justice, not to refuse to the Devil domination over human kind, whom he had subjected to himself by his evil counsels. For indeed it would have been unjust that the Devil should not have dominated those of whom he had taken possession. . . . Man was delivered over to the watchman of death until the death of the flesh. . . . The Devil was moved by the perverse desire to harm us: nevertheless, he acted conformably to *his strictest rights*. God decided that his power should subsist until the day when he should kill a righteous man in whom he could find nothing worthy of death, because this Righteous One should be killed without having committed a single sin, and even without having been born under the law of concupiscence. Until then, the Devil would hold mankind *by virtue of a* not unlawful right of possession. It is therefore very justly that the Devil is constrained to release those who believe in Him Who was killed most unjustly. . . . It was not by violence that man was released from the Devil, who had seized him by persuasion and not by violence.'

The thought that inspires these texts is this: in consequence of Adam's sin, in which all participated, men were beneath the dominion of the Devil, who put them pitilessly to death. God had power to ruin this dominion by means of violence. But in that case, justice would have been outraged, seeing that the dominion of the Devil over mankind was in accordance with right. God found a way to overturn, without violence and in conformity with the laws of justice, the tyrannical rule under which we groaned. This is how it was done. The Devil put Christ to death as he had put to death all the rest of mankind. Now Christ had not committed any personal sin. His birth itself had not been defiled by concupiscence. Free of all sin, He did not belong to the dominion of the Devil. And the Devil, when he put Christ to death, overstepped his rights. He paid for this abuse of power by the loss of all dominion over those who believed in Christ: a most just punishment for a most unjust crime. Christ, in presenting Himself to the Devil clothed in human nature, laid a snare for our gaoler, who foolishly allowed himself to be caught in it. Christ vanquished the Devil by a stratagem which was legitimised by a

state of war. But He vanquished him without violence and without departing from the laws of justice.

This is what Saint Gregory the Great says about
it : in the *Morals*, 33, 16-31, Gregory comments on
the text of *Job* xl. 19, where the Vulgate makes God
say that Behemoth (the crocodile) is taken with a
fish-hook. . . . This is his text :

' Who does not know that, in a fish-hook, the
bait is shewn, while the barb is hidden ? For the
bait attracts and the barb pricks. This is why our
Lord, coming for the redemption of mankind,
made Himself, as it were, into the fish-hook to kill
the Devil. For He took on a body to lead this
Behemoth to accomplish the death of the flesh,
which was the bait. In seeking unjustly the death
of the body, the Devil lost us whom he had held
justly. He was taken with the fish-hook of the
Incarnation because, when he threw himself upon
the bait of the body, he was pierced by the barb
of the divine. There was the humanity destined
to attract the glutton ; there was the divinity
which was to transfix him. . . . He was, then, taken
by the fish-hook because what he had devoured
killed him. This Behemoth knew, doubtless, that
the Son of God was incarnated, but he did not
know the plan of our Redemption. He knew that
the Son of God was incarnated for our Redemption ; but he was completely unaware that this
Redeemer would transfix him as He died. (Behemoth now bears the name of Leviathan, 17.) This
Leviathan was taken with a fish-hook ; for while,

through the intermediary of his satellites, he bit at the bait of the body in our Redeemer, the barb of divinity transfixed him (the fish-hook is furnished with a line which is composed of the ancestors of the Saviour). The hook remained in the throat of the glutton and it bit him who bit it. (30, Behemoth—Leviathan is compared to a bird.) The Lord caught him, as a bird is caught, by showing him the bait of the Passion of His only Son, but hiding the snare from him. . . . It was meet that the death of sinners dying justly should end by the death of the Just dying unjustly.'

In another place in the *Morals*, 17, 47, we see the Devil attacking the body of Christ ; then we read :

' He was vanquished in the very place where he had power to act, and from that power which he had received to kill exteriorly the flesh of the Lord, it came about that his power over us was killed. Exteriorly the victor, interiorly the vanquished. And he who, of right, held us debtors to death, of right lost his right of death over us, because he undertook, through the intermediary of his satellites, to slay the flesh of Him in Whom he found nought of the debt of sin. Our Lord thus paid the tribute of death which He did not owe, in order to stop death, of whom we were debtors, from slaying us. . . . (The Devil because he killed Christ) lost of right Him Whom, so to say, he held justly.'

Dominion of the Devil over men ; dominion exercised in putting men to death ; dominion vested with a juridical character; eviction of the Devil consequent upon the abuse of power which he committed by putting to death one exempt from fault; thus, an eviction conforming to the laws of justice. That is what Augustine had said; that is what Gregory repeats in these texts. He explains to us that Christ, not having sinned, was not a tributary of death, and that the Devil, on the day when he crucified Christ, committed an injustice for which he was punished by losing his dominion over us.

CHAPTER XVI

CHRIST OVERTHROWS THE DOMINION OF
THE DEVIL IN HELL

BY putting Christ to death, the Devil fell stupidly into the snare which was prepared for him: he lost his dominion over mankind. But now we must note that the disaster which Satan had to suffer was even more profound, and that, beginning upon earth, it had its prolongation in hell.

Christ, after His death, descended into hell. Upon this point we have the witness of the Apostles' Creed, where we read:

' Was crucified, dead and buried; He descended into hell.'

And the teaching of the Creed is confirmed by several very ancient writings, notably by the *First Epistle of St Peter* (iii. 19).

In hell Christ consummated the work of the redemption. Upon what then came to pass, several of the Fathers, but above all the *Gospel of Nicodemus,* composed in the third century, have left us precious information. Let us collate them.

Saint Cyril of Jerusalem says in the *Catecheses,* 14, 19:

' Death (the Devil) was frightened when he saw the arrival of this person upon whom the bonds of hell had no hold. Why, guardians of the kingdom of shadows, were you seized with terror? Death fled, and this flight betrayed his fear. The holy patriarchs on the contrary, pressed forward: Moses, Abraham, Isaac, Jacob, David, Samuel, Isaiah and John the Baptist, who asked him: "Art thou He who is to come, or must we await another?"'

Saint Chrysostom thus expresses himself in the homily: *Against the Jews concerning the Divinity of Christ*, 5:

'When Christ had descended into hell, he threw it into disorder and confusion; he overthrew the fortress. This was foretold by David when he said: "Open your gates, O princes! Open, O eternal gates and let the King of Glory enter in!" The same thing was predicted by Isaiah in these words: "I will throw down the gates of brass, I will shatter the bars of iron: and I will give thee the treasures of darkness and hidden riches of secret places." It is thus that he depicts hell. He spoke of treasures because hell then held saintly souls, precious vessels, that is to say: Abraham, Isaac and Jacob. But these treasures were hidden because the sun of justice had not yet bestowed upon them its light.'

In the homily: *On the Sepulchre and the Cross*, 2, delivered on Good Friday, the same doctor says:

'To-day the Lord has made the round of hell, after breaking in pieces the doors of brass, and cutting asunder the bars of iron. It is said, not that he opened the doors of brass, but that he broke

H

them in pieces, so that henceforth the prison is useless. The Lord of angels descended into hell, and there showed forth his might. First he bound the strong one therein, then he seized his riches. . . . When a king has seized a captain of brigands who lived by pillage and gathered his booty into his cavern, he binds him and delivers him up to torture : as for his booty, he carries it to the royal treasury. This is what Christ did. By his death he bound the captain of the brigands, the guardian of the prison, that is to say, the Devil. Then he carried to the royal treasury all his riches, that is to say, the human race.'

Among the Latins, Rufinus, in his commentary : *Upon the Apostles' Creed*, 16, gives us the following text, of which Saint Chrysostom and Saint Gregory the Great were later to make use :

' The fish which swallows the hook concealed beneath the bait does not detach the bait from the hook, but he is drawn from the depths of the water to serve as food. In the same way, he who possessed the empire of death in truth drew into death the body of Jesus without seeing that under this bait was concealed the hook of divinity. But when he had devoured it, he became at once inert. The gates of hell were broken, and he was torn from its depths to serve as prey. . . . The divine nature of Christ descended into death by the intermediary of the flesh, not to be retained by death as are mortals, but to open the gates of death. As when a king enters a prison, opens the gates, breaks the chains, cuts asunder the bars, gives back their freedom to the prisoners, and light and life to those who were in darkness and in the shadow of death.'

Now let us pass to the *Gospel of Nicodemus.*

This book, probably written at the beginning of the third century, presents (chapter 17) Carinus and Leucius, sons of the aged Simeon spoken of in the *Gospel of St Luke.* These two men were dead. But Jesus, the vanquisher of death, associated them with Him in His resurrection. Thus they came forth from the tomb, and lived in the town of Arimathea. They were taken to Jerusalem and asked to relate the miracle of which they were the beneficiaries. Then they said (18 *et seq.*) :

'While we were, with all our fathers, in the shadows, we were suddenly enveloped in a light brilliant as the sun, and a kingly effulgence illuminated us. Immediately Adam, the father of the human race, the patriarchs and the prophets, spoke in a transport of joy: " This light, it is verily the author of the eternal light, who has promised to light us with a light that shall not fade." The prophet Isaiah cried, "It is the light of the Father, the Son of God, according to my prophecy when I was on earth." Our father Simeon, radiant with joy, approached us and said to us all : " Praise the Lord Jesus Christ, the Son of God ! I received him into my hands in the temple when he was new-born. . . ."

'And while all the saints were full of joy, Satan, prince and captain of death, said to the prince of hell, " Make ready to receive Jesus, who pretends to be the Christ, the Son of God, and who is a man fearing death, for he has said : ' My soul is sad unto death.' For he frequently opposed me and many men whom I had made blind, lame, deaf, or lepers, and whom I had tormented by divers demons, he healed them with a word. And those whom I had brought to you dead, he took them back from you."

' And the prince of hell, answering Satan, said : " Who is this prince so powerful and who yet feareth death ? . . . Who is this Jesus who, fearing death, opposeth thee ? If he is so puissant in his humanity, truly I say unto thee he is all-powerful in his divinity, and none can resist his power. And when he says that he fears death, he seeks to deceive thee. And evil will be upon thee throughout eternal centuries."

' Satan, prince of death, answered and said : " Wherefore dost thou hesitate to take this Jesus, thine adversary and mine ? For I tempted him, and I excited against him mine ancient people, the Jews. . . . I made ready the wood to crucify him and nails to pierce his hands and feet. His death is near, and I will bring him to thee, yielded to thee and to me."

' The prince of hell answered and said : " Thou hast said that it is he who wrested the dead from me. Many are here whom I still hold. While they lived on earth, they took the dead from me, not by their own powers, but by the prayers which they addressed to God ; their all-powerful God seized them from me. What then, is this Jesus who, by his word, has taken the dead from me? It is perhaps he who, by his imperious word, brought back Lazarus to life. . . ."

'Satan, prince of death, answered and said: "It is this same Jesus."

'The prince of hell, hearing this, said to him: "I conjure thee, by thy power and mine, bring him not to me. For when I heard the power of his word, I shook with terror, and my impious ministers trembled with me. . . . This man who has been able to accomplish these things is the strong God and he is the Saviour of the human race. If thou bringest him to me, he will deliver all those whom I hold here, shut into prison, and chained by the bonds of their sins. He will lead them, by his divinity, to the life which shall last as long as eternity."

'While Satan and the prince of hell were conversing thus with one another, a voice was heard like thunder and the storm, saying, "Princes, open your gates! Open, ye everlasting doors! And the King of Glory shall come in."

'The prince of hell, hearing this, said to Satan, "Get thee gone and go forth from my realms. If thou art a puissant king, fight against the King of Glory. But what is there of likeness between him and thee?" And the prince of hell threw Satan forth from his realms. And he said to his impious ministers: "Shut the gates of brass; fasten the bars of iron and resist valiantly; lest we be reduced to captivity, we, who keep the captives."

'But when they heard this, the saints said to the prince of hell with reproachful voices, " Open thy gates and let the king of glory enter."

'David, the divine prophet, cried, " Did I not prophesy, when I was on earth, that the mercies of the Lord would render witness unto him and that his marvels would foretell him to the sons of men ? For he has broken in pieces the doors of brass and cut in sunder the bars of iron."

'Another prophet, Isaiah, also said to the saints, " Did I not foretell, when upon earth, that the dead would awaken ? I said also : Death, where is thy victory ? where is thy sting ? ' "

'All the saints, hearing these words of Isaiah, said to the prince of hell : " Open thy gates ; vanquished and overthrown, thou art now powerless."

'And a voice like thunder said : " Princes, open your doors ! Open your everlasting doors ! And the king of glory shall come in."

'The prince of hell, hearing this cry for the second time, said, as if he were ignorant of it : " Who is this king of glory ? " David, answering the prince of hell, said, " I know those words. . . . The Lord, strong and mighty, it is he who is the king of glory. . . . And now, base prince of hell, open thy gates and let the king of glory enter in ! "

'While David spake these words to the prince of hell, the Lord came upon them in human form. He illumined the eternal shadows, he broke the bonds that held us, and an indomitable power of

God visited us, we who sat in the darkness of sin and in the shadow of death.

' When they beheld this sight, the prince of hell, Death, and their impious ministers, were seized with terror. Crying out to Christ, who was there in their midst, surrounded by dazzling light, they said, " Thou hast vanquished us ! Who art thou, thou whom the Lord sendeth for our confusion ? "

' And all the legions of demons, filled with the same terror, cried out, " Whence art thou, Jesus, thou man so puissant, and of such majesty ? . . . Who art thou, thou that, without fear, hast crossed the boundaries of our domains ? . . . Art thou that Jesus of whom Satan, our prince, said that, by thy death upon the cross, thou wouldest receive limitless power over the whole world ? "

' Then the king of glory, in his majesty, trampling death underfoot, seized Satan and destroyed his power and brought back Adam to the radiance of the light.

' Then the furious prince of hell said to Satan : " O Beelzebub, prince of damnation . . . what hast thou sought to do ? Thou wishedst to crucify the king of glory. . . . Dost thou now see thy folly ? Behold this Jesus dissolves all the shadows of death by the effulgence of his divinity. . . . Behold, those who groaned beneath our torments insult us. . . . Our dominions are overthrown, and we no longer inspire the race of men with terror. . . . Those who, from the beginning until now, had despaired of salvation and of life, are no longer heard to groan. . . . O Satan, keeper of the keys of hell, now thou hast lost by the wood of the cross those riches which thou hadst acquired by the tree of the fall. . . . Thou shouldest first have sought a just reproach to make to this Jesus! Since thou didst not find in him any fault, wherefore hast thou dared to crucify him unjustly, and to bring here among us the righteous and the just? Thou hast lost the evil and the impious of the whole world."

' And, as the prince of hell thus spake to Satan, the King of glory said to the prince of hell: " Satan shall be beneath thy dominion throughout the eternal centuries, instead of Adam and his sons, who are my righteous ones." '

CHAPTER XVII

THE TRUE ORIGIN OF THE DEVIL

BEFORE going further, let us stop a moment before this drama, whose first act unrolled upon Calvary, and whose *dénouement* was in hell. Christ fought with the Devil a battle which the Catholic liturgy does not hesitate to call a duel:

> 'Mors et Vita duello
> Conflixere mirando.'

sing the faithful at High Mass on Easter Day. And, without doubt, Christ came out the victor from this duel. But at what price? He had first to let Himself be crucified by His terrible adversary, and death was the ransom of His triumph. And the Fathers explain to us that this death was necessary, and why it was so. Executioner of the human race, the Devil was also its master. His empire over mankind had a juridical basis, which had to be respected by God Himself. Under penalty of violating the laws of justice, God could not drive out our tyrant save after having led him to commit an abuse of his powers, to overstep his rights. On the other hand, the Devil could not overstep his rights save by killing Christ who, though clothed in human shape, was not beneath his dominion. And, since the Devil would not have been stupid enough to put Christ to death voluntarily and

121

designedly, Christ had no other resource to lead our executioner to commit an abuse of his powers than to disguise His identity and to present Himself to the Enemy as an ordinary mortal ; in short, to lay a snare for him, and to have recourse to ruse.

Who, then, is this mysterious personage who has rights even *vis-à-vis* God, with whom God treats as one power to another, and whom He could only drive out by means of a ruse ? The information given us by the Fathers excites our curiosity without satisfying it. But let us read, in the letters of Ignatius of Antioch, chapter xix of the letter to the *Ephesians*. There we learn that God, manifesting Himself in human form, appeared one day in the sky like a marvellous star, in order to destroy sorcery, abolish ignorance, overthrow the ancient kingdom, shatter the bonds of evil and begin to destroy death. We learn further, that the apparition of the divine star, which took place in the despite of the prince of this world, produced a universal consternation. Like the God of the Ignatian letters, the Christ of the Fathers came to abolish ignorance, overthrow the ancient kingdom, shatter the bonds of evil and destroy death. Like Him, also, He used ruse towards the prince of this world. Both pursued the same object ; both had recourse to the same procedure. An intimate link connects them. Now the God of the Ignatian letters is the good God who, hidden beneath the veil of an ethereal body, came down from the third heaven upon earth, in order to tear mankind from the cruel dominion of the Creator ; He is in disguise because the Creator would not have let Him traverse the lower sky, where he is master, if he had had knowledge of His passage, for he would have been on his guard if he had suspected the ruin with which he was menaced.[1] Now we have the explanation of the Devil. This perverse being is the evil God of dualist metaphysics, who was surreptitiously introduced into Catholic belief, and who, obliged to adapt himself to monotheist doctrine, transformed himself into a creature revolted against God. Unknown to the Old Testament, he penetrated into the New Testament about the year 150, and his first apostle among the Fathers is Saint Justin.[2] The Devil of the Fathers is a mutilated being, and suffered a second amputation on the day when Saint Anselm expelled him from the dogma of the Redemption.

[1] Delafosse, *Lettres d'Ignace d'Antioche*, p. 74.
[2] *Id., Les écrits de Saint-Paul*, I, 24–38 ; II, 18–26 ; I, 22–24 ; 28, 108 ; IV, 93 ; *Le Quatrième Evangile*, pp. 19–26.

PART FOUR

ACTIVITIES OF THE DEVIL SINCE THE FOUNDATION OF THE CHURCH

The Devil crucified Christ; but, following upon this crime, he was stricken with destitution, and deprivation of his rights, and his empire over mankind vanished; this is what the texts have told us. Nevertheless, even after his defeat, the Devil has remained the great evil-doer; he has not ceased to injure the human race. How are we to reconcile the former idea with the latter? We must recognise frankly that no reconciliation is possible. We are confronted with an irreducible antinomy. But one cannot make one step in the domain of theology without coming up against some contradiction. Instead of wasting our time in recrimination, let us simply say that, in spite of the ruin of his empire over the human race, the Devil has nevertheless continued to persecute men. We must now recount his misdoings. The material is abundant: a selection is necessary—and a classification.

Sometimes the Devil has let loose the plagues of nature; at other times, his activity has been confined to the world of humankind. Let us observe that he has always sought to injure mankind. But, in the first case, he has reached them indirectly and by rebound, by overturning the material world that God has put at our service. In the second case, he has struck directly at mankind, and spared the inferior creatures. In short, the evil-doing of the Devil has been manifested in two domains, and the evils with which he has loaded the human race fall into two general groups.

CHAPTER XVIII

THE DEVIL IN NATURE

SAINT AUGUSTINE teaches in *De Doctrina Christiana*, 2, 35, that:

> 'The lower part of the world, that which we inhabit, has been subjected to the false angels by the law of divine providence, to which the magnificent order of things is due.'

Before him Origen had developed the same thought, which seems to say the opposite, since he attributes the government of the world to the good angels (*Contra Celsum*, 8, 31):

> 'We believe that nothing is done without the help of invisible labourers and ministers. . . . But we do not think that these invisible ministers are demons. Strictly speaking, if these demons play any rôle here, that which we must attribute to them is famine, the sterility of trees and vines, excesses of heat, the poison in the air which destroys fruits, kills animals and brings plagues upon men. The authors of these evils are the demons whom the divine justice uses as executioners, and to whom it sometimes gives the power to do these things, it may be in order to stimulate the conversion of men given to vice, it may be to try the pious. . . .

The Psalmist is our witness that the divine justice
sends us calamities by the intermediary of bad
angels. He says, in fact (*Psalm* lxxviii, 49), that God
used the bad angels to discharge his anger upon
men. . . . The law of God has not confided the
government of the earth to any demon ; but the
demons, in consequence of their impiety, have
perhaps cast their pretensions upon certain lands,
in which there is ignorance of God and of the kind
of life pleasing to God, or in which the enemies of
God abound. Perhaps also the Word which orders
all things has confided the government of men who
are evil and rebellious against God to these beings,
who are worthy to guide and to chastise the evil.'

Tertullian teaches us just how far the hold of the
Devil extends over the creatures of nature in this
passage from *De Baptismo*, 5, where, after describing
the rôle of water in pagan rites, he adds :

' But, apart from all rites, do not the wicked
spirits live in the waters, in order to imitate the
act accomplished by the Divine Spirit at the beginning of the world ? . . . Let us then not doubt
that the holy angel of God is there to adapt the
waters to the salvation of men, while the bad angel
uses this element for man's downfall.'

And this opinion of Tertullian's has become that
of the Church which, even to-day, exorcises water
and salt before using them in its service. Luther,
upon this point, preserved the doctrine of the
Church, as is proved by this passage from his

LUCIFER DEVOURS JUDAS

Satan is represented with a triple face. While the
mouth in front is devouring Judas, each of his
side mouths devours a demon

THE DEVIL CARRIES OFF A WITCH

nature, the Devil does not forget mankind. He leads them into sin : he makes his dwelling in their bodies, to torment them at his ease. He fears not, from time to time, to gratify upon them his instincts of lubricity. At other times, having made infamous pacts with them, he grants them extraordinary powers. Let us review the different branches of this varied, but always evilly designed, activity.

Chapter XIX

THE DEVIL INDUCES MEN TO SIN

THE *First Epistle of St Peter* warns the Christians that the Devil tries to detach them from the faith and to throw them into heresy; it conjures them not to let themselves be taken by his snares in this celebrated text (v. 8):

> 'Your adversary, the Devil, as a roaring lion, walketh about, seeking whom he may devour; whom withstand stedfast in your faith. . . .'

The same thought is found in the following passage from the *Epistle to the Ephesians* vi. 11:

> 'Put on the whole armour of God, that ye may be able to stand against the wiles of the Devil. For our wrestling is not against flesh and blood, but against . . . the world-rulers of this darkness. . . .'

And it is again as the principle of error that the Devil is described in this passage from the *Second Epistle to the Corinthians* iv. 3:

> 'But and if our gospel is veiled, it is veiled in them that are perishing: in whom the god of this world hath blinded the minds of the unbelieving, that the light of the gospel of the glory of Christ, who is the image of God, should not dawn upon them.'

That is, the sin to which the Devil in the New Testament persuades men is the sin of the Spirit, the sin against faith, that is to say, heresy or infidelity. With Irenæus, Satan, without ceasing to be the principle of error, also urges men to infraction of the laws of morality. That is what the following text teaches us (4, 24, 3):

'The Devil, who is the rebellious spirit, can do nought but what he did at the beginning, that is, seduce the spirit of man, make him transgress God's commandments, blind hearts and incline them to forget the true God and adore himself as a God.'

It is the same with Tertullian, who says in his *Apologeticus*, 22:

'All the operations of demons tend toward the ruin of men. . . . And since the beginning, their malice has been fierce against men. . . . Demons and angels corrupt souls, precipitate them into anger or folly, inflame them with evil passions, blind them to the point of making them adore themselves, and cause to be offered to their statues sacrifices and perfumes with which they regale themselves.'

In the book *Exhortation to Martyrdom*, 2, Saint Cyprian teaches us that the Devil seeks to draw Christians into apostasy. He says:

'Is not the first object of the Church to hearten against the attacks of the Devil, by frequent exhortation, the people whom God has confided to

us and the army established in the celestial en-
campment ! It is against the ancient enemy that
we are fighting. The Devil has been attacking
mankind for nearly six thousand years ; with the
passage of time he has learnt to vary his temptations, his artifices, and his snares. When he meets
a soldier of Christ unprepared, ignorant and confused, he makes use of his experience and he
deceives him.'

Little by little, the seduction of the spirit was
relegated to the second place, when it was not left
aside altogether. The rôle of the Devil consisted
mainly, or even uniquely, in drawing men away from
the moral law. This is what we read in the *Catecheses*
of Saint Cyril of Jerusalem, 2, 31 :

' Thou art not the only author of sin ; there is
another being who bears thee towards it ; it is the
Devil. He suggests sin to all ; but he is powerless
over those who have no friendliness for him. He
inflames the passions of those who follow him. It
is from him that there comes adultery, fornication
and sins of every kind.'

Saint Gregory the Great discourses at length in
his *Morals* upon the ravages caused by the Devil,
whom he speaks of under the name of Behemoth, in
the Christian world. He says (33, 12) :

' It is, indeed, not at all astonishing that Behemoth, before the water of baptism, before the
heavenly sacraments, before the Incarnation of the
Redeemer, should have swallowed up the river of
the human race in the gulf of error. What is sur-

prising, what is terrifying, is that he has had many victims even since the Redeemer, that the water of baptism does not preserve from his defilement, that the heavenly sacraments do not stop him from feeding hell. . . . It was mere play for the Devil to carry off the unfaithful. His whole effort is devoted to enticing into death those whose generation causes him so much suffering. Wherefore, we must not think that faith without works suffices. We must not think that it suffices to profess the faith in order to escape from the tooth of Behemoth. . . . Doubtless, faith has preserved us from his jaws, but let us beware lest we should be thrown upon them by our actions.'

The learned even came to ask whether Satan was not the immediate cause of every sin committed on earth. Among those who gave affirmative answers to this question, we must note Saint Leo the Pope. This is what he says (*Sermon*, 9, 1) :

'When any man whatever commits any sin whatever against God, it is through the deceitfulness of the Devil that he has been seduced. It is through this perverse being that he has been corrupted.'

But this doctrine harmonises badly with the dictum of *St James* (i. 14), where we learn that each is tempted by his own covetousness. Besides, if human nature is corrupt, vicious, as was admitted since Saint Augustine, how did we need the intervention of Satan in order to do evil ? We fall into sin by our own weight, without the Devil taking part ; the Augustinian doctrine of Original Sin logically tended to suppress as useless the rôle of the Devil in temptation. Naturally, the demands of logic were not rigorously adhered to. Nevertheless, some concessions were made to them, and it is admitted that covetousness of the flesh is the single cause of certain sins. It is this that Saint Gregory means in his *Morals*, 11, 64 :

> ' The temptation of impurity does not come from outside ; it comes from our own depths. It gnaws the flesh like a moth fretting the garment from which it comes forth. Man bears within himself the cause of his temptations.'

Saint Thomas teaches, in his *Summa*, 1, 14, 3, that temptation is not always the work of demons. His view has been generally adopted.

CHAPTER XX

THE POSSESSED

Possession is the state of a person in whom the Devil dwells, who is his plaything, whom he possesses. Very numerous, throughout the centuries, were the victims of possession by Satan. Some of them had virtues or genius which have made them immortal in history: we will speak of them later. Here we will treat of the mass, from whom we will take a few examples, in chronological order.

The *Acts* relate (xvi. 16) that St Paul, during his stay at Philippi encountered:

'A certain maid, having a spirit of divination, which brought her masters much gain by sooth-saying.'

We shall see later on that the apostle exorcised this young woman. Here we will content ourselves with establishing that there were possessed persons at the time of St Paul. It was even a common thing, to judge by another text from the *Acts*, where we read (xix. 13):

'But certain also of the strolling Jews, exorcists, took upon them to name over them which had the evil spirits the name of the Lord Jesus, saying, I adjure you by Jesus whom Paul preacheth.'

136

The same conclusion is to be drawn from the texts in which Saint Justin, Saint Irenæus and Tertullian celebrate the marvellous exorcisms by the Christians. Their testimony will be cited later. For the moment, it suffices that there were, in the time of these doctors, possessions, and numerous possessions. We must add, possessions which belonged to the pagan world, for the Fathers only spoke of pagans. But one may ask how the idea of demoniacal possession came to a pagan, who had no knowledge either of the Devil or of the demons of Christianity ? The answer to this question is furnished by the following text from Saint Justin (1 *Apol.*, 18, 4) :

> ' Men seized and shaken by the souls of the dead, whom all the world calls demoniac and raving.'

Whence it follows that the pagans knew ' demoniacs,' and they called by this name persons who were the prey of disordered agitation. The way in which Justin explains this agitation is not that of the Christians, it is that which he attributes to the pagans.[1] But let us remember that possession is a fact prior to Christianity. What is Christian, is the interpretation of the fact.

In his book *Contra Celsum*, 8, 34, Origen alludes to demoniacal possession, when he notes that Christians are not subject to it and that pagans alone are its victims :

> ' We know that there are many demons on the earth, and we attribute to them great power over

[1] The pagans ascribed nervous diseases sometimes to the gods, sometimes to the spirits who, since Hesiod, were called *daimon*, demon.

evil-doers, who deliver themselves up to them through wickedness (36). Let Celsus not think to frighten us by threatening us with the harm that the demons may do us, for we despise them. For the demons which we despise can do nothing against us, for we are protected by God, who is able by Himself to defend those who are worthy of His help. Nevertheless, God charges His angels to defend His faithful.'

Saint Cyprian describes the activity of the demons in these terms (*Idola non dii*, 7):

'They disturb life, give nightmares. After introducing themselves furtively into bodies, these spirits terrify souls. They torture the limbs, destroy health and bring about illnesses.'

Heretofore, the possessed whom we have met with have been pagans; for the delivery up to Satan of the incestuous man of Corinth, of which the *First Epistle to the Corinthians* speaks, has a special meaning, and does not refer to a possession.[1] In his book *De Lapsis*, 24, Saint Cyprian speaks of a woman who

'having become wicked, and being seized by a wicked spirit, tore out her tongue with her teeth, and died shortly afterwards.'

This woman, seized by 'a wicked spirit' was certainly possessed. Now she had received the grace of the baptismal bath, and she had defiled this grace by sacrificing to idols in order to escape persecution. Thus she was a Christian. We have here the first

---

[1] Delafosse, *Les Ecrits de St Paul*, 2, 27.

example of a Christian person possessed by the
demon. Henceforth, only possession of Christians
will be mentioned.

In the *Life of Saint Hilary*, 21, related by Saint
Jerome, there is mention of a ' virgin of God ' who,
having opened her heart to passion, gave herself up
to unbridled acts. These phenomena were the result
of a demoniacal possession, for when the girl was
brought by her parents to Saint Hilary :

> ' The demon began to howl and cry : " I am
> being hurt ; It is against my will that I am brought
> here." '

Towards the end of the fourth century, the monk
Vigilantius protested against certain practices of
Christian people, and notably against the worship
given by the faithful to the bones of the martyrs.
Saint Jerome saw in the attitude of Vigilantius the
influence of demoniacal possession, and he pointed
out to him the way to cure himself (10) :

> ' I see, thou miserable one, what thou fearest.
> The wicked spirit that maketh thee write these
> things hath often been tormented by this vile dust
> (of bones of the martyrs) : it is still to-day.
> Through thy mouth it dissimulates, but through
> the mouth of others (who are possessed) it avows
> openly. . . . This is the counsel I give thee. Enter
> into the basilica of the martyrs and thou wilt be
> cured. There thou wilt find many of thy com-
> panions (who are possessed). Thou wilt be
> scorched, not by the candles that so much displease

thee, but by invisible flames. And then thou wilt
avow what now thou deniest, thou wilt proclaim
that through the mouth of Vigilantius, it is Mercury who speaketh.'

Saint Augustine mentions, in the *City of God*,
several healings of demoniacs. His texts will be cited
later. Here I would simply point out that he knew
cases of possession. In the *Genesi ad Litteram*, 12, 35,
there is mention of one possessed who, at a distance
of twelve miles, saw a priest who was a friend of his
and followed his steps. However, Augustine, though
inclined to see in that a case of diabolical possession,
is not absolutely certain. He says :

> ' This man was perhaps only a madman ; but,
> because of these phenomena, he passed as being
> under the power of a demon.'

About the year 830, the church of Uzès was the
scene of singular phenomena. Those who entered it
felt convulsions and burnings. Agobard, Archbishop
of Lyons, when consulted about this, perceived in
these doings the act of the Devil, who seeketh in all
things and everywhere, to harm the faithful.[1] Fifteen
years later, phenomena no less strange took place at
Dijon. The faithful who entered this church were the
prey of movements disordered to the point of making
them roll on the ground. When consulted by Bishop
Theotbald, Amolon, Agobard's successor to the See
of Lyons, spoke, he too, of diabolic possession, but
not without excluding the hypothesis of fraud :

[1] Letter to Barthelemy of Narbonne.

'Has anyone ever seen, in the churches of God
or at the tombs of the martyrs, miracles of this
kind, which do not tend to heal the sick, but to
strike down and to send quite out of their minds
those who were well ? . . . How can we fail to per-
ceive in this the artifices of a few perverse men or
the illusions of demons ? '

Saint Bernard several times encountered demoniacs
upon his path and he accomplished upon them exorcisms of which we shall speak later.

From the fifteenth century onwards, demoniac
possessions acquired a frequency which they had
never had before. Indeed, they often presented themselves in epidemic character, and one possessed person
communicated his disease to those around him. At
Loudun, for instance, where the Superior of the Ursulines was tormented by the Devil, several nuns of
her community were the prey of similar torments.
Protestant communities were spared as little as
Catholic. At Friedeberg in Saxony the Devil suddenly took possession of more than sixty people of
every age and both sexes and he tortured them frightfully. The prayers prescribed by the Consistory
obtained no result, and the number of the possessed
rose to 150. This took place in 1594. At the same
date, at Spandau, the demon took possession of more
than forty people, of whom the greater part were
young boys and girls.[1] Naturally, the Protestant
ministers explained to their flock that the Devil, the
great enemy of God, would not thus savagely fall

[1] Janssen, *L'Allemagne et la Réforme*, 6, 439.

upon the ' Evangelicals ' if he regarded them as servants, and that these possessions were, in fact, the best proof of the truth of the Reformation. As the Catholics used the same argument, there was rivalry —in Germany—between Catholics and Protestants as to which should have the greatest number of possessed.

Chapter XXI

Illustrious Victims of Possession

SATAN has not limited himself to the seduction of common people, or those already corrupted. Even elect souls have not escaped his evil instincts. Numbered among his victims in antiquity are Saint Antony and several of the Fathers of the desert. In modern times we have Saint Theresa, Father Surin, the Curé of Ars, now canonised. And the Church of Rome has not had the monopoly of these trials, for Luther, too, had to undergo the assaults of the demon.

§ 1. Saint Antony and the Fathers of the Desert

Antony, the great anchorite, whose extraordinary virtue attracted so many monks into the desert of the Thebaid, had to sustain the assaults of hell. Saint Athanasius relates what the Devil did to induce Antony to sin (*Life of Saint Antony*, 5, 6):

' He harassed him during the night, and he persecuted him sometimes to such a point that Antony took up the posture of a wrestler. The Devil sent him obscene thoughts; Antony repulsed them by his prayers. The Devil made himself tender and

143

caressing; Antony, shamefast, protected his body
by faith, prayers and fasts. The Devil took the
form of a woman; he reproduced her gestures.
But Antony remained faithful to Christ. . . . He
who thought to be able to make himself like God
was vanquished by an adolescent. He who thought
himself above flesh and blood was wrecked against
a man clothed in flesh and blood. . . . Finally, the
dragon, seeing that he could not overthrow Antony,
was seized with rage. He appeared to Antony as
he is in reality, that is, in the form of a black
child: ceasing to attack by thought alone, he took
a human voice and said: " Many are they whom I
have deceived, whom I have thrown down: but I
have been able to do nothing against thee." Antony
asked him, " Who art thou—thou who speakest
thus?" The Devil replied in a groaning voice,
" I am the friend of fornication. I lay my snares
before the young to make them fall into this vice,
and I am called the spirit of fornication. . . . It is
I who have tormented thee so many times and have
always been repulsed." Antony, after giving thanks
to God, replied to his enemy, confidently: " Thou
art utterly contemptible; thy spirit is black and
thou art like a child without strength. Henceforth
I will disturb myself no more because of thee, for
the Lord is my help and I can despise my enemies."
When he heard these words, the black man fled at
once and did not even dare come near this man.'

Palladius who, from 386 to 412, was in contact
with the monks of Palestine, and above all with those

THE TEMPTATION OF ST ANTHONY
St Anthony is represented as being lifted in the air
by the demons

of the body. Having gone out and wandered about in the desert, I found the lair of a hyena. I decided to go in without any clothing, in order to be devoured by the beasts when they came out. . . . I was not devoured. I concluded that God had pardoned me, and returned to my cell. Then, after being quiet for several days, the demon assaulted me yet more violently than before, to the point of being near blaspheming. He transformed himself into a young Ethiopian girl whom I had formerly seen gleaning. Then this young girl sat herself on my knees, and excited me so much that I believed I was having commerce with her. Filled with rage, I slapped her and she became invisible. . . . Filled with discouragement, I wandered in the vast desert. I found a small asp and, taking it up, I applied it to my genital parts, in order to be bitten and thus to achieve death. And having crushed its head against the organ which was the cause of the temptation, I was not bitten. Then a voice, penetrating my spirit, said to me, " Go forth, Pakhon, and fight. For I have delivered thee up to temptation precisely in order that thou shouldst not have pride as if thou wert strong and in order that, conscious of thy weakness, thou shouldst put thy trust in the help of God, instead of in a way of living." Reassured, I retraced my steps. From that moment onwards, I have passed my life in peace, without worrying any more about this war. The Devil, seeing that I despised him, has not come near me again.

' (Upon Evagras). The Devil of concupiscence

importuned him mightily, as he himself relates. He passed his nights in a well; it was the depth of winter and his flesh froze.

'I will say a few words about the brother who has been with me since my youth. . . . He has been tried more than a thousand times by demons. One day the demon proposed the following bargain to him: " Agree with me to sin just once, and I will bring thee any woman thou wilt point out." Another time, having struggled with him for fourteen nights and pulling at his foot, he said to him: " Do not adore Christ and I will not come near thee." But he answered: " I do adore him, and I shall continue to adore him, precisely because it gives thee so much annoyance." '

§ 2. LUTHER

Travellers who visit the castle of the Wartburg, near Eisenach in Saxony, go into the room where Luther lived after the Diet of Worms, and are there shown on the wall the blot of ink in front of which thousands of pilgrims, for four centuries, have stood with religious respect. The monk who had revolted against the Pope and the Emperor was busy upon a translation of the Bible. One evening he saw the Devil who, as if hung upon the wall, appeared to him with grimacing face and mocking laugh. In a fury, he threw the inkpot at his head; hitting the wall, it left there the famous blot.

This tale is only a legend. Luther never threw an

inkpot at the Devil's head. But, at the Wartburg and elsewhere, he was often at grips with Satan. This is what he says in his *Table Talk*, VI, 6816, Weimar edition :

'In 1521, when I was in my Patinos, I was living isolated from the world in a small room. No one could come to see me there except two servants who twice a day brought me food and drink. They had bought me a bag of nuts, and I shut them up in an old cupboard and ate a few from time to time. But one evening, when I had just extinguished my light and lain down, lo and behold ! my nuts began to dance. They were shaken about, they were thrown against the panels with a hellish noise all around my bed. I had not asked one question, nor said one word, when, as I was going to sleep, behold, a racket on the staircase, as if a succession of barrels were being tumbled down it. Yet I knew that everything had been shut with chains and bolts and that no one could have come up. Yet the barrels continued to roll about. I rose and went to the staircase to see what was happening. Then I said : " It is thou ! Very well, then, get out ! " And I commended myself to the Lord Jesus.'

In the same *Table Talk*, IV, 5097, we find :

' The Devil throws hideous thoughts into the soul—hatred of God, blasphemy and despair. These are the great temptations and not one Papist has understood them. These idiotic asses know only the temptations of the flesh. Those are the only ones about which they and their saints have written. One day, pursued by a temptation of that kind, Benedict threw himself naked among the thorns, and conscientiously tore away his————— In reality, the remedy for that particular temptation is easy; there are still women and girls. But in temptations of blasphemy and the thought of the Judgement of God one cannot see where the sin begins nor where to find a remedy.'

During the day, thanks to work and distractions, Luther managed to keep Satan's suggestions from his spirit. But at night the battles redoubled in violence, as the two following avowals prove:

' When I awake at night, the Devil tarries not to seek me out. He disputes with me and makes me give birth to all kinds of strange thoughts. I think that often the Devil, solely to torment and vex me, wakes me up while I am actually sleeping peacefully. My night-time combats are much harder for me than in the day. The Devil understands how to produce arguments that exasperate me. Sometimes he has produced such as to make me doubt whether or no there is a God.'

Naturally, Satan was the advocate of the Church of Rome, and reproached Luther with his revolt against the Pope:

' The Devil begins by saying : " Who has commanded you to preach the Gospel? Who has given you the mission to preach thus, as no bishop, no saint, has thought fit to preach it for so many centuries? How would it be if God should disapprove of you and if the loss of all the souls that you have seduced and made stray should fall upon you?" Satan would have given me far more trouble if I had not been a doctor. But that I was a doctor, he would have killed me with this argument: "You have no mission!" When the Devil finds me lazy and losing sight of God's word and neglecting to arm myself with it, he throws confusion into my conscience, accusing me of teaching error and introducing division into the Church, that was so peaceful and so calm under the Papacy, and of having engendered scandal by my doctrines. The Devil understands marvellously well how to torment us: "Oh, indeed," he says, "you preach the Gospel! And who has commanded you to do it? who has given you the mission?"'

But Luther, shaken for a moment, always ended by taking hold of himself again. He hurled a storm of foul curses at Satan, which put the enemy to flight.

§ 3. SAINT THERESA

At the order of her confessor, Saint Theresa recounted the graces with which her celestial spouse, Christ, overwhelmed her: also the trials which she had to undergo. Thus we read in Chapter XXXI of her *Life* (Bouix I, 423):

'After speaking of certain temptations and certain inner and secret troubles which came to me from the demon, I now wish to relate others with which I was assailed almost publicly and wherein his action was visible. One day I was in an oratory when he appeared to me, on my left side, in frightful form. While he was speaking to me, I particularly noticed his mouth. It was horrible. From his body there came forth a great flame, clear and unmixed with any shadow. He said to me in a terrifying voice that I had escaped from his hands, but he knew well how to seize me again. Great was my fear. I made as I best could the sign of the cross. He disappeared, but returned at once. Put to flight by a second sign of the cross, he tarried not to return again. I did not know what to do. Finally, I threw some holy water towards where he was, and he came back no more. Another day, he tormented me for five hours by pains so terrible, and by such frightful anguish of body and spirit that I thought I should be unable to resist any longer. It is my custom, in these moments of intolerable suffering, to commend myself to God, and to perform, interiorly, acts of resignation. I ask God for the grace of patience, and then I accept, if it is for his glory, to remain in this state until the end of the world. Thus I sought by this method to find some alleviation of the cruel torment that I endured, when it pleased the Lord to make me see that it came from the demon. For I saw near me a little nigger of horrible form, who ground his teeth in despair because he was sustaining a loss just when he thought to have made a gain. I began to laugh, and was fearful no longer. But the Sisters who were with me were seized with terror and did not know what to do, nor what to apply to remedy such great torment. The Enemy unleashed himself against me in such terrible fury that, by an irresistible movement, I struck myself great blows upon my head, my arms and all over my body. To crown my suffering, I was delivered up to interior anguish even worse, which left me no single instant of rest, and I did not dare to ask for holy water for fear of alarming my companions, and letting them know whence my anguish came.

I have many times proved that nothing equals the power of holy water to chase away demons and prevent their return. They fly, too, at the sight of the cross, but they return. The virtue of this water must indeed be great ! For my part, I taste a very special and very perceptible consolation when I take it. Commonly it makes me feel a renewal of my being that I cannot describe, and an inner pleasure that fortifies all my soul. That is not an illusion : I have proved it very many times and I have given the greatest attention to it. I can only compare so agreeable an impression with that refreshment of his whole being which is felt by he who, exhausted with heat and thirst, drinks a glass of cold water. And this makes me think of the quality of greatness with which the Church impresses everything she establishes. I tremble with joy when I see the mysterious force which her words communicate to the water and the astonishing difference which exists between that which is blessed and that which is not,

'As my torment did not cease, I said to my nuns
that, if they would not laugh at it, I would ask for
holy water. They brought me some, and threw it
over me : but that had no effect : I threw some
myself towards where was the spirit of darkness,
and instantly he departed ; all my pains left me as
if they had been lifted from me by a hand. But
I remained shaken and broken as if I had been
beaten all over with a stick. A very useful lesson
had been given me. I could form an idea of
the tyrannical dominion exercised by the demon
over those who are in his power, since he can,
when God permits him, torture to such an ex-
tremity a soul and a body which do not belong
to him.

'A little while ago, I beheld myself taken with
the same fury ; but the torment was not so long.
I was alone. I took some holy water and hardly
had I thrown it than the Tempter disappeared. On
the instant there came in two nuns, exceedingly
worthy of belief, who would not have told a lie
for anything in the world. They smelt a very bad
smell, like sulphur. As for me, I did not smell it at
all. But, according to their testimony, it lasted
long enough to give me the opportunity of perceiving it myself.

'Another time, when I was in the choir, I fell
suddenly into the most profound state of con-
templation. I went out, in order that no one should
be aware of this. At the same time, the nuns heard
heavy blows in the place near where I had withdrawn ; and I heard near me loud voices, and it

seemed to me that some plot was being hatched. But only a confused noise came to my ear, because I was too deeply absorbed in the oraison. So that I felt no fear. . . .

' About the same time, I thought one night that those evil spirits were coming to suffocate me. A great quantity of holy water was thrown at them, and suddenly I saw a great multitude fleeing away, as if they were throwing themselves from the top of a rock. Now I have no fear of them, knowing that without the permission of the Lord, they cannot make the least movement. . . . As it would take too long to speak of them all here, I will content myself with relating what happened to me one evening of All Souls.

' I was in an oratory, and I had just recited a nocturne : I was saying a few very devout oraisons which are at the end of our breviary when the demon placed himself on the book, to stop me finishing them. I made the sign of the cross and he disappeared : he came back almost immediately, and I put him to flight in the same way : it was three times, I think, that he obliged me thus to begin the oraison again. Finally, I threw holy water at him and I was able to finish. I beheld in that very instant several souls come forth from purgatory, who doubtless had little more still to suffer : it entered my thoughts that this enemy had perhaps by that delayed their deliverance. I have rarely seen him in any form, but frequently without one, as happens in those intellectual visions of which I have spoken, where one sees clearly, without any form striking the eyes of the soul.

'I want to relate another thing which astonished me very much. On the day of the feast of the most Holy Trinity, having entered into an ecstacy in the choir of a certain monastery, I beheld a great battle between demons and angels without being able to understand the meaning of this vision. I knew it clearly when, about fifteen days later, there broke out a great battle between certain of those who say oraisons and a great number of others who live strangers to this holy exercise. . . . Another time I beheld myself surrounded by a multitude of these enemy spirits : but I was at the same time invested with a bright light, which prevented them from coming right up to me. I understood that God was protecting me against them and that they could not lead me into any sin. I have since had divers proofs of the truth of this vision.'

§ 4. SŒUR JEANNE DES ANGES, SUPERIOR OF THE URSULINES OF LOUDUN

Jeanne de Belcies, daughter of a baron of Saintonge, entered, in 1622, the community of the Ursulines who, a few years later, set her at the head of their house at Loudun. At that time there was no other talk, in this little town save of the curé of the parish of Saint Peter, Urbain Grandier, and of the number-less victories which this seductive and sensual ecclesiastic had won over the virtue of women.

Jeanne des Anges—that was her name as a nun—whose days were passed in great part in the *parloir*, soon learnt what all the world knew. Her imagination was ardent, she became violently interested in the curé of Saint Peter's, of whom she spoke endlessly to her nuns, and she asked him to confess them at the convent. Grandier, who found sufficient game in the town, refused this new hunting-ground. Then Jeanne became the victim of a mysterious malady. Demons who, according to her formal declarations, were sent by Grandier, tormented her frightfully. Several of her nuns suffered similar tortures. That was the origin of the affair of Loudun (1632). We shall see later the tragic *dénouement* it had for Grandier. What interests us here is solely the state into which the demons threw Jeanne des Anges when they had taken possession of her person. Jeanne, by order of her superior, related her trials. And her story which, in the words of Charcot, 'is distinguished amongst all by a very special character of truth and sincerity,' was published towards the end of the last century.[1] Let us collate the information which she gives us :

'(p. 62) I gave scarce a thought to Our Lord. . . . On the contrary, I spent my time in the parlour. . . . If my sisters had not been good nuns, my bad example would have put them in great danger of losing their souls. . . . (p. 64) By this time, Our Lord permitted that evil should be

[1] G. Légué and G. de la Tourette, *Sœur Jeanne des Anges* (avec préface de M. le Professeur Charcot), Paris, 1886. It is from this book that the following extracts are taken.

thrown upon our community by a priest named Urbain Grandier, priest of the principal parish of the town. This wretch made a pact with the Devil to ruin us, to make us into women of bad life. In order to do this, he sent demons into the bodies of eight nuns of this house, to possess them . . . the effect was such that all the nuns of this community were afflicted by it, some by possession and some by obsession, and that in less than fifteen days. . . . (p. 65) The demons in an exorcism made feint to leave my body and give up their place to God. They were six months without appearing, but they insinuated themselves little by little into my spirit, and into my inclinations, so that they . . . made me one with them: they bound me so strongly by their passions that I was full of their feelings. Each of the seven demons whom I had in my body took the position which he considered he could the best maintain. . . . (p. 67) During this time the priest of whom I have spoken employed the demons to excite in me love for him : they gave me desires to see him and speak to him. Several of our sisters had the same feelings without communicating them to us. On the contrary, we hid them from one another as best we could. After the demons had thoroughly excited in us the passion of love for this man, he failed not afterwards to come at night into our house and into our rooms to solicit us to sin.

‘ (p. 68) When I did not see him, I was consumed with love for him, and when he presented himself to me, and wished to seduce me, our good

God gave me a great aversion for him . . . it is true that I have been faithless in combating the impure thoughts and movements which I felt . . . I say with truth to my great confusion, that I gave great hold to the Devil by my bad habits . . . for if I had truly studied myself for the mortification of my passions, the demon would never have caused such disorder within me. (p. 69) Thus I had seven demons in my body, of whom the chief was Asmodeus. His operation was ceaseless within me, as much in my imagination as in my mind, which he filled with shameful things. Modesty prevents me from describing them in detail, for they are strange.

' The second demon was Leviathan. . . . When he was in my head, I wanted to put everything in order, but with such pride that it seemed to me that everything ought to bow beneath my laws and that the earth was not worthy to support me. I behaved with my sisters in a most imperious way. . . .

' (p. 70) The third demon was called Behemoth. His operation in me was to oppose himself to every action that concerned the worship of God in my soul. Often I had my mind filled with blasphemies, and sometimes I uttered them without being able to make any reflection to prevent myself. . . . I felt a continual aversion against God, and I had no greater object of hatred than the sight of his good-ness. . . . It is true that, by the mercy of God, I was not free in these feelings, although then I did not know it, for this demon blinded me in such a way that I could scarcely distinguish his wishes from my own. Moreover, he gave me a very strange aversion to my profession as a nun, so that sometimes, when he was in my head, I tore up all my veils, and those of my sisters which I could find. I crushed them under foot, I ate them, cursing the hour when I had entered the cloister. All this was done with great violence. I think I was not free.

' (p. 72) The spirit of these wretches and mine became one thing, so that through their influence, I took on their feelings, I wedded all their interests, as if they had been mine. I would indeed have wished to do otherwise, but I could not accomplish it. . . . (p. 73) The fourth of these evil spirits was called Isacaaron. He was of the same trade as Asmodeus for impurity. Those who have directed me know the pains which this unhappy being gave me. His passion was violent and as if enraged. There was this difference between that of Asmodeus and his, that the first acted rather by way of insinuation, while Isacaaron went to extremes and blinded reason. . . .

' The fifth was called Balaam. His passion was all the more dangerous because it seemed less evil. He only troubled my imagination a little, and then he let my nature act. . . . (p. 74) I was not able to distinguish so well the passions of the two other demons, all the more because they were chased out first of all when I had enough liberty to understand what they were doing with me. They were called Gresel and Aman.

' Our ills appeared so great externally, and the disorders into which the demons threw us were such that several eminent persons had compassion upon us. I was put under the direction of Father Recollet, called Gabriel Lactance. . . . This good father had great dominion over the devils. . . . In less than six or seven weeks he chased three demons from my body, that is, Asmodeus, Aman and Gresel, and this in the presence of Monseigneur de Poitiers and more than six thousand people.

' (p. 75) Monseigneur de Poitiers gave us four friars, who worked with great assiduity and fervour over our possessed sisters. Father Lactance, having had such success by the retreat of the three demons mentioned above, continued to exorcise me with a great deal of assiduity from the month of May to the month of September, when God sent him a great sickness, of which he died. . . .

' (p. 79) (One day, when she was discontented with Father Lactance, the thought came into her head that the demon could well humiliate him.) I was so miserable that I did not resist that thought sufficiently strongly. When I presented myself for communion, the Devil took hold of my hand and, after I had received the blessed Host and had moistened it, the Devil threw it in the priest's face. I know well that I did not do this action in freedom, but to my great confusion I am fully certain that I gave the Devil power to do it, and that he would in no way have had this power if I had not connected myself with him. . . .

' (p. 80) Isacaaron, who was the one that

[*Photo: Musée de Sculpture*

THE NOVICIATE THEOPHILUS MAKES A PACT WITH THE DEVIL

From a pillar of Chartres Cathedral

operated the most in me and gave me scarcely any relief, took great advantage of my cowardice, in order to give me horrible temptations against chastity. He carried out an operation upon my body, the strangest and the most furious that can be imagined. Then he persuaded me that I was big with child, so that I believed it firmly, and I had all the signs of it that one can have.

'(p. 88) As I did not describe my temptations (to the confessor), they increased more and more, so that there grew in me such despair because of the state in which I was, and principally of the anxiety which I had about this apparent bigness, that I came to a decision to make myself die. . . . I determined to take a certain brew, and to do this I found a way to obtain drugs. But as our good God did not wish to ruin me, he gave me a great fear for the loss of the soul of the little creature who, I thought, was in my womb. And so I took the decision not to use these drugs, and I threw them away.

' (p. 89) I made another altogether diabolic plan, which was to make an opening in my side, to draw out this child, which I would baptise, and thus his salvation would be assured. I saw clearly that I would put myself in danger of death; I thought that I ought to put myself in a good state for it. . . . I therefore prepared myself to confess as rigorously as I possibly could, without, however, revealing to my confessor this plan. On the day after my confession, which was the second of January, 1635, I went into a little closet, with the intention of

L

carrying out my plan, and of opening my side.
I carried with me a large knife, and water to baptise
this little creature who, I thought, was in me. I
began to undress in order to accomplish my design
more easily. . . . I made a great opening in my shirt
with scissors. After which I took the knife which
I had brought with me, and began to bury it
between my two ribs near the stomach. . . . But
instantly I was thrown down to the ground with
a violence I cannot describe. . . . Very distinctly
I heard a voice say : " What thinkest thou to do ?
Desist from thy evil design. Have recourse to thy
Saviour and convert thyself to Him, for he is near
thee to receive thee."

(p. 98. In the course of the following weeks,
Jeanne saw Father Surin come to her in the middle
of the night, take her hand and press it in sign of
friendship. Then, a little later) '. . . I heard a voice
which said to me : " It is no time now to resist ; since
God has subjected you to a certain nature, you are
obliged to content it on such pressing occasions."
Then I felt impressions of impurity in my imagination and disordered movements in my nature. . . .
At other times during the night it was said to
me . . . " You ought to reveal to him whom you
love the passions that you have for him, and per-
suade him to content you."

'(p. 101. How did the matter of the bigness
find its *dénouement ?*) The external state in which
I was made the superior powers depute a prelate
with doctors to find out what was happening to
me. I will not describe what passed—the *procès-*

verbal is witness. I will tell only one external thing which helped me a great deal to convert myself to God, which gave me great confidence in his compassion : it is that the holy Virgin compelled this unhappy spirit who had undertaken to make me pass for pregnant to declare his wicked designs in the exorcisms. He was constrained to make me give up by my mouth all the masses of blood that he had collected in my body. That took place in the presence of a bishop, of doctors and of a number of other people, who praised God and the blessed Virgin with us. Thus I remained wholly free from all these pains, and the external signs of bigness disappeared at the same time.

'(pp. 103-135. Nevertheless, Jeanne experiences horrible temptations when Father Surin is near her. This Father, who knows them by supernatural revelation, reassures his penitent.) (p. 135. Jeanne has just said that she has fought with Leviathan.) The second demon whom I undertook to fight was infamous Isacaaron. His operation consisted in giving me ceaselessly a feeling of needles stuck in my flesh. . . . This enemy of all purity did abominable things to me almost every night. p. 138) To defend myself against these passions, I had nearly always my scourge in my hand. Often I took it up seven or eight times a day, and for a long time each time. During that year, I never took it less than three times a day, and with such violence that I was ordinarily covered with blood. During the extreme cold of winter I have passed parts of the night undressed in the snow or in tubs

of icy water. Beside that, I often went among
thorns, so that I was all torn by them. At other
times I rolled in nettles, and there passed whole
nights defying my enemies to attack me. . . .

'(p. 168. Jeanne and Father Surin begin a
novena to obtain the expulsion of Balaam.) The
latter sought every device he could to prevent me
continuing my novena. To achieve this, Behemoth
and he seized my head. . . . Then it came about
that these demons foresaw the hour of mass and
made me breakfast with such desire that I ate more
at that time than three famished people. . . . If
ever anyone was afflicted, it was I. . . . I felt myself
intensely urged to say to Father Surin that he
should command the demons in the name of God
and Saint Joseph to make me throw up all that
I had taken. Father Surin did so. Shortly after,
the demon returned into my head, from which he
had a little retreated, and afterwards he suddenly
made me vomit with such abundance that it was
inconceivable. The Father esteemed that I ought
not to fail to communicate. Therefore I approached the holy Table with a great tenderness
of devotion. And thus I continued my novena
up to the end. In the last days Balaam appeared
in the exorcisms with an absolutely extraordinary
fury. He made me bite my hand very cruelly,
howling like a dog. . . .'

To give a brief résumé of the rest of the memoir :
One day, when Jeanne seemed to be dying, and her
doctor himself had lost all hope, she was instan-

taneously healed by Saint Joseph, who appeared to
her with shining face and anointed her on her diseased
side. And the demons, when they finally left her
body, impressed on her hand the names of Jesus,
Mary and Joseph. These holy names, which all could
see, and which nothing could efface, were a sensible
and material proof of divine intervention. The
unction of Saint Joseph was another, for a few drops
of this celestial balm remained on the shirt of the
healed one, so that all could see them and re-aspire
their perfume. Jeanne, provided with this evidence,
went, with the authorisation of the bishop and all the
king's government, as a pilgrim to the tomb of the
blessed François de Sales at Annecy. It was a
triumph. Everywhere on her journey the people
gathered in crowds to gaze upon the shirt that had
been the depository of Saint Joseph's unction and the
hand upon which the names of the Divine Family
stood out in relief. The shirt was an object of venera-
tion, for it performed miracles. But its prestige was
nothing beside that of the hand. It was this, above
all, that they wished to see; it was round it that they
thronged with an ever-new curiosity. The greatest
personages were no less eager than the people. The
Cardinal of Paris, Richelieu, Anne of Austria, Louis
XIII, without mentioning numerous bishops, wished
to see the prodigy.

Richelieu, who was then ill, said to Jeanne, when
he received her at his bedside : ' I feel very grateful
to God for having let me know your innocence in the
midst of the cloud of calumnies with which you were
charged. . . . It is a stroke of God's special Providence

He has wished, by all that has happened, to sanctify those who have been troubled by demons ; and it is even for the general good of France, which draws such great benefit from it. . . . There is no need for greater proof of the truth of possession than the continuation of this store of holy names which are renewed with such brightness whenever God judges it necessary to operate. These are sensible testimonies of real possession and of the great designs which God had when he permitted them.'

After these words Richelieu took the miraculous shirt into his hands. Here I will let Jeanne speak (p. 223) :

.' Although he was ill, he uncovered his head, he smelt at it (the shirt) and kissed it twice, saying : " That smells marvellously good." He touched it with a reliquary which he had at the head of his bed.'

Anne of Austria was expecting a child, who was going to be Louis XIV. She thought that the shirt honoured by the favours of Saint Joseph would procure her a happy delivery, and she asked that she should be given a bit of it. But Jeanne explained that the shirt was called to work many conversions, and that it was necessary to keep it whole.

§ 5. FATHER SURIN AND THE CURÉ OF ARS

Father Surin, a Jesuit of great virtue, intervened, after the torture of Urbain Grandier, in the affair of Loudun, and exorcised the Superior of the nuns. He obtained remarkable results, but the Devil revenged himself cruelly upon his vanquisher. Here is the letter which the unhappy Father, who had become the plaything of the demons, wrote on the 3rd of May, 1635, to Father d'Attichy, a Jesuit of Rennes. It has been published by Aubin, on page 217 of his book : *Histoire des diables de Loudun* :

'There is scarcely anyone to whom I take the opportunity to relate my adventures save Your Reverence, who hears them willingly, and has thoughts about them which would not come easily to others who do not know me as you do.

'Since the last letter that I wrote to you, I am fallen into a state far from what I had foreseen, but well agreeing with God's Providence for my soul. I am no longer at Marennes, but at Loudun, where I received your letter a little while ago. I am in ceaseless conversation with the devils, in which I have had a history which would be too long to recount to you, but which has given me more cause than I ever had to know and wonder at the goodness of God. I want to say something about it to you, and I would say more to you if you were more discreet. *I am entered into combat with four demons*, among the most powerful and malicious in hell : *I*, I tell you, whose infirmities you know well. God has permitted that the combats have been so violent and the attacks so frequent that exorcism has been the least of the fields of war : for the enemies have declared themselves in secret, night and day, in a thousand ways.

'You can imagine for yourself what delight there is in finding oneself at the mercy of God alone. I will say no more to you of that. It suffices me that, knowing my state, you will take action to pray for me. Things are such that, for three and a half months, I have never been without *a devil near me and active*.

'Things have gone so far that God has permitted, I think for my sins, what has perhaps never been seen in the Church, that, in the exercise of my ministry, the Devil passes from the body of the possessed person and coming into mine, assails me and overthrows me, troubles me and visibly traverses me, for several hours possessing me like a demoniac. I am unable to explain to you what passes in me during this period, and how this spirit unites with mine without taking from me either the intelligence or the freedom of my soul, while nevertheless making itself as if a second me and as if I had two souls, of which one is dispossessed of its body and of the use of its organs, and holds itself apart and looking on at the one which has come in. The two spirits fight in a field which is the body, and the soul is as if divided. According to one part of oneself, it is the subject of diabolic impressions, and according to the other, of movements which are proper to it, or which God sends to it. . . . I feel the state of damnation and I apprehend it, and I feel myself as if pierced with the thrusts of despair in this alien soul which seems to be mine. And the other soul, which is full of confidence, mocks at such feelings and in all liberty curses him who causes them. Often I feel that the same cries that come from my mouth come equally from these two souls, and I am troubled to discern whether it is joy that produces them or whether it is the extreme fury which fills me. . . . When I want, through the movement of one of these two souls, to make the sign of the cross upon my mouth, the other turns away my hand with great speed and seizes my finger between my teeth and bites me with rage. I scarcely ever find an oraison easier or more peaceful than in these agitations, while my body reels about and the ministers of the Church speak to me as to a devil, and load me with maledictions. . . . When the other possessed people see me in this state, it is a pleasure to see how they triumph, and how the devils mock me, saying : " Physician, heal thyself! Go now, ascend into the pulpit ; how good it will be to see him preach after rolling about all around. . . ."

' Some say that it is a chastisement of God upon me in punishment for some illusion : others say something or other else : and I am unmoved and would not change my place with any other, being firmly persuaded that there is nothing better than being reduced to great extremities. I am in such a state that I have little freedom of action. When I wish to speak, my words are stopped ; at Mass, I am stopped short too, at table I cannot put a piece of food in my mouth ; at confession, I suddenly forget my sins ; *and I feel the Devil come and go in me as if in his own house.* As soon as I wake, he is there; at oraison he takes away my thoughts when he pleases; when my heart begins to swell, he fills it with rage; he makes me sleep when I wish to watch; and publicly through the mouth of the possessed woman, he boasts that he is my master; to which I have nothing I can say in contradiction. . . . *It is not only one demon that works in me. There are ordinarily two of them.* One is Leviathan, who is opposed to the Holy Ghost: all the more that, as they have said here, in hell they have a trinity which the magicians adore: Lucifer, Beelzebub and Leviathan, who is the third person in hell. Some authors have noted and written of it before. . . . Now the operations of this false Paraclete are all contrary to the true, and impress upon one a desolation that cannot be adequately described. He is the chief of the whole band of our demons and he has the superintendence of this whole business, which is one of the strangest that have, perhaps, ever been seen. We see in the same place Heaven and Hell: nuns like the Ursulines taken in one way and in another worse than the most base, fallen in every kind of disorder and filth, blasphemy and furious error.

'I do not want Your Reverence to make my letter public, if you please. You are the only one to whom, apart from my confessor, and my superiors, I have wanted to say so much. It is only to keep up some communication which may help us to glorify God, in whom I am your very humble servant.—JEAN-JOSEPH SURIN.'

The state described here with such remarkable precision was prolonged for twenty years. It even became worse ; for the Devil left his victim only rare moments of lucidity : and one day he threw him violently through a window of his room. In his fall poor Father Surin broke a leg. The invisible persecution ended, nevertheless, by leaving him in peace. And before his death the pious Jesuit recovered the use of his faculties.

§ 6.   THE CURÉ OF ARS

The famous Curé of Ars, who died in 1859, and is to-day inscribed by the Roman Church in the catalogue of the saints, waged a fierce war against the Devil, who revenged himself cruelly but in vain. This is what his latest biographer relates (Germain, *Le bienheureux Vianney*, p. 88) :

‘ Our blessed one had filled the cure of Ars for six years when the enemy of God began to torment him during the night. At first he contented himself with knocking at the door of the courtyard, as if he wanted to break in, then at an inner door ; but soon he penetrated right into the curé's room and there abandoned himself for several hours to making terrifying noises. From that time on, he came back every night. The curé was extremely terrified, at the beginning, to such a point that he nearly fell ill. The Grappler [1]—this, as every one

---

[1] ‘ Le Grappin ’ in the original.—*Translator's note.*

knows, is what he called the demon—imitated, either around his bed or in some other part of the house, the whole gamut of all the noises most calculated to disturb sleep. He gave the illusion sometimes of a charge of cavalry or of the passing of a troop of soldiers; sometimes of the walk of a heavily-shod man or of the bounds of a maddened horse or again of the stepping of a flock of sheep. Another time he produced the deafening clang of a hammer driving in nails. Every imaginable thing that is frightening or unpleasant, he did. . . . Finally, he disdained not to have recourse to jugglery. He lifted the blessed curé from his bed. . . . It was in the course of these attacks of rage that he threw his victim on the floor and, to afflict him, broke the fount that was near him and besmeared with filth the picture of the Holy Virgin in the presbytery.

'These mysterious happenings were very soon known to the outer world, and many received them doubtfully. In general, the members of the clergy refused to admit the reality of the diabolic manifestations. But . . . several trustworthy witnesses heard these noises, which were inexplicable on natural grounds. . . . Other witnesses heard a noisy visitation which was inflicted on the valiant apostle outside his parish in 1826. . . . The sound of steps was heard on the staircases and in the bedchambers: and then, on several occasions, pieces of meat were found in the soup on fast-days. . . .'

CHAPTER XXII

LICENTIOUS DEMONS

THE Devil, not content with persecuting his victims, even took a shameful pleasure in dishonouring women, in unloosing demons, who slaked upon them their lubricity. The monk Gilbert of Nogent declares (*De vita sua*, 3, 19 end) that he could say many things on this subject : but he does not relate them, for fear of frightening his readers.

The monk Arnold, who was more expansive, and who lived in the entourage of Saint Bernard, tells us the following happening, in which his illustrious friend was concerned (*S. Bernardi vita*, 2, 34) :

(St Bernard, accompanied by the bishop of Chartres, has just arrived at Nantes.) ' In this part of the country there was an unhappy woman tormented by a demon. This lascivious being lit in her the fires of passion and stretched himself out upon her and treated her as a spouse after passing one of his hands under her body, and the other under her head. An invisible adulterer, he came in the night, while the woman was lying near her husband, who knew nought, and he abandoned himself to lust upon her. For six years this wickedness remained hid, and the unhappy woman revealed her shame to none. However, in the

seventh year, the spectacle of her continued crimes
and the thought of the judgements of God terrified
her. She sought out the priests and avowed her
opprobrium. Then she went on pilgrimages and
implored the help of the saints. But pilgrimages,
confessions and prayers obtained no result. The
demon returned every day and became more and
more licentious. The crime at last became known
and the husband was furious. At this juncture the
man of God (Bernard) arrived in the country. As
soon as she heard of his coming, the woman went
and threw herself at his feet, trembling. She told
him everything, and explained that she had vainly
carried out the instructions of the priests. The man
of God spoke to this woman gently, promised her
the aid of Heaven and, as night was falling, he told
her to come back on the following day. Early on
the following morning the woman returned : she
reported to the man of God the blasphemies which
her incubus had uttered in the course of the
previous night, accompanying them by threats.
The man of God said to her : " Do not be upset
by these threats, but take my staff, put it in your
bed, and we shall see what it will do." The woman
carried out this injunction. She went to bed, after
making the sign of the cross, and she placed the
staff near her. The demon presented himself immediately, but he could not abandon himself to
his customary labour, for he did not even enter
the room. But he uttered violent threats and
declared that, once the man of God had departed,
he would resume his practices. The man of God

told the bishop (of Nantes) to gather together all the people of Nantes in the church on the following Sunday. When Sunday came, he ascended the pulpit and, before preaching, he prescribed that all present should hold lighted candles in their hands. Then he related the unheard-of transgressions of the Devil: he hurled his anathema upon the lascivious spirit who had abandoned himself to frightful defilements contrary to nature. All present supported this anathema: finally, he enjoined upon him, in the Name of Christ, not to approach this woman nor any other. As soon as the sacramental candles were extinguished, the power of the Devil was completely destroyed. The woman confessed herself and then communicated: the Enemy never appeared again, but departed for ever.'

Cæsarius of Heisterbach, a monk of the thirteenth century, relates divers stories concerning incubus demons, from among which I select the following:

' *Miraculorum*, 3, 8: A priest named Arnold had a daughter whom he loved greatly and whom he protected with jealous care against the enterprise of young men, and particularly of the canons of Bonn, for she was very beautiful. Whenever he was out, he shut her up in the loft of his house. One day the Devil appeared to the girl in the shape of a man and lit in her the fire of passion. The unhappy girl let herself be seduced, and from that moment on, she abandoned herself to the demon. One day the priest, coming up to the loft, found his daughter in tears. After first refusing to reveal the cause of her sorrow, she ended by admitting that she had been seduced by the demon. The stricken father made her go across to the other side of the Rhine, hoping that, at the same time this would calm her and would draw her from the incubus demon. When the girl had departed, the demon appeared to the priest and said to him in a loud voice: " Wicked priest, wherefore hast thou ravished my bride from me ? Thou shalt pay me for this ? " And instantly he struck him so violent a blow on the chest that the priest died after three days, vomiting blood. This history was told me by the abbot of my monastery, and by my brother the monk Gerard, who was then a student at Bonn. They both knew all about it.

' 3, 9 : The following affair, which took place twelve years ago, I have from my brother the monk Arnold, who witnessed it. In the burg of Brisecke, near the field of Rinecke, a woman had allowed herself to be seduced by the demon. One day, being suddenly overcome with weakness and perceiving that she was on the point of death, she asked for a priest. She admitted to him that for several years she had been the plaything of the demon and had had infamous commerce with him. She had admitted this to none, either because she did not dare or, more probably, because she was enslaved.

' 3, 10 : A certain John was a student at Prüm. This is what is related about this man, who was

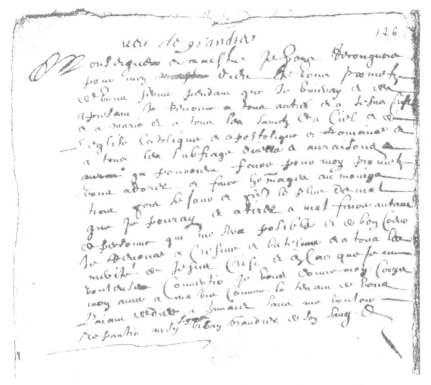

[Photo: Grillot de Givry

AUTOGRAPH OF THE PACT OF URBAIN GRANDIER

(A translation is in the List of Illustrations)

IDEM IMPETRAVIT A DEO VT MAGVS A DEMONIBVS DISCERPERETVR

[Photo: Grillot de Givry

DEMONS TEAR A MAGICIAN TO PIECES ON THE COMMAND OF ST JAMES

a doctor but a libertine, and what was told me by my abbot. A woman had promised to spend the night with him. The night came, but not the woman; but the Devil, taking on the form and voice of the woman, climbed into the clerk's bed and he, thinking he had affair with the woman, carried out the conjugal act. When morning came, he told the pretended woman that she must go. The latter then said to him : " With whom do you think you have been lying ? " He replied that he had slept with such and such a woman. " Not at all," said the demon, "it is with the Devil that you have been lying." Utterly nonplussed, John bawled at the Devil an oath which I am ashamed to repeat.

'3, 13 : At Bonn, a town in the diocese of Cologne, a priest named Peter, curate of the parish, hanged himself by a secret judgement of God. Filled with terror, his concubine, whose name was Alheyde, renounced the world and entered a nunnery. One day, when she was in the dormitory, she saw through the window a young man, near the adjacent well. As soon as he perceived her, this young man, who was in reality a demon, climbed up the curb of the well, and, reaching the window, he seized Alheyde and tried to carry her off. She was terrified and cried out and fell, half dead. The sisters, having heard her cry, ran to her and put her into her bed. Then they left her. When he saw that she was alone, the demon came back again and entreated her to do evil. She, understanding that she had affair with a wicked

M

spirit, refused. The demon said to her : " Good Alheyde, give me your consent, and I will procure for you a rich and honest husband. Why stay in this wretched house, to die of hunger and kill yourself before your time ? Return to the world, take your part of the delights which God has created for men. With my protection, you shall not want anything." Alheyde replied : " I regret that I followed you for so long a time. Get thee gone, for I wish to serve you no more." Then the demon blew his nose in a disgusting way. Nevertheless, he ceased not to harass her night and day. The sisters counselled Alheyde to keep holy water near her, and to sprinkle herself with it, or to burn incense, if the holy water did not succeed. She employed these devices, but without great success. Doubtless, when the demon saw the sign of the cross, the holy water and incense, he withdrew, but he tarried not to return. A more experienced sister counselled Alheyde to let the demon approach ; then to cast at him, full in face, the angelic salutation, uttered aloud. The counsel was put into execution. Then the demon, as if he had been pierced by an arrow, or borne away by a hurricane, fled, and from that moment he never dared come near her again. Armed with this arrow, the nun had no more cause to fear the demon. She spoke of it one day to a monk, who said to her : " Make a general confession to your Prior of all the sins which you can remember, and you will no more be troubled by demons." She obeyed and, having arranged with the prior, she went to the place fixed for the confession, the chapel adjacent to the monastery. The demon appeared to her on her way, and tried to lead her astray, and followed her right to the place where her confession was to take place. When, at the feet of the prior, she began her confession, the demon uttered a groaning cry and disappeared for ever. There you have a manifest proof of the power of confession. I have this information from my lord Hermann, abbot of Saint Mary's, who had known this woman at Bonn when he was a canon, and who, having gone to her monastery, gathered from her own lips the tale of all these happenings.'

In 3, 6, we read the story of a young girl of Nivelles, in Belgium, whom the demon pursued with his assiduities, and whom he ended by persecuting, without managing to shake her virtue. I will confine myself to selecting the following statement :

'The young girl said : "Each time that he has come towards me, he has so managed that I have never been able to see his back."'

Cæsarius' questioner seeks what motive the demon can have had to have acted thus, to which Cæsarius replies :

'Another vision has told me that demons have no posterior side.'

In 3, 12, Cæsarius teaches us that the Goths, in the course of their passage from Asia to Europe, abandoned all their women who were ugly, in order not

to compromise the purity of their race. Then he
adds :

> ' These unhappy women wandered through the
> forests, and were assailed by incubus demons. The
> products of these unions gave birth to the nation
> of the Huns.'

CHAPTER XXIII

SORCERERS AND WITCHES: THEIR EXISTENCE

BY the name of magic or sorcery, we mean the power of producing effects which surpass human powers. The holders of this power which, naturally, emanated from the Devil, were called magicians or sorcerers. Doubtless, the possessed and the demoniacs did things beyond the power of man, but they were only passive and unconscious instruments of the Devil, who happened to be tormenting them especially. But the magicians or sorcerers themselves exercised the powers that Satan had given to them. They were the agents of the Devil, and not his instruments; and the pact or contract which bound them to the Prince of darkness was the same as that which binds the agent to his master.

The Old Testament relates two cases of magic. The first is furnished by *Exodus* (vii. and viii.), where we read of the exploits accomplished by the magicians of Egypt at the time of Moses. These men changed rods into serpents; they transformed the water of the Nile into blood; they produced frogs which invaded Egypt. In short, they accomplished several of the wonders accomplished by Moses. Nevertheless, they did not accomplish them all, and they were vanquished. It could not have been otherwise, for God, who had confided His power to Moses, had not confided it to the magicians of Egypt.

The second case of magic is related in the *First Book of Samuel* xxviii. 7-20, where the witch of En-dor, upon Saul's demand, makes Samuel's soul appear.

Here let us make an observation. The wizards of Egypt, the witch of En-dor, possessed powers superior to human strength. From whom did they hold them? The Biblical texts, which tell the exploits accomplished by these persons, do not say. Later on, the Fathers will explain to us that the wonders of Egypt, like the prodigy of En-dor, were illusions of the Devil. The Bible itself is silent. It is only since the epoch of the Fathers that the magicians have become the associates and collaborators of Satan.

In the course of his first missionary journey, the Apostle Saint Paul encountered, in the isle of Sala-mina, the sorcerer Bar-Jesus or Elymas, and he smote him with a temporary blindness, not without first copiously cursing him, and, in particular, calling him a ' Son of the Devil.' Saint Paul knew Satan who, for him, was the Roman Empire, and of whom he speaks at the end of the *Epistle to the Romans;* but he did not know the Devil. It is only in the middle of the second century that the epithet ' Son of the Devil' was introduced into his speech to Elymas.

In the *Apologeticus*, 22, 23, Tertullian speaks of the demons and magicians in these terms :

' Wherefore cite the prodigies of these deceiving spirits; the phantoms that reproduce the forms of

Castor and Pollux, the water that a vestal bears in a sieve, the vessel which another vestal draws with her girdle, the beard which becomes suddenly red? All these wonders have been accomplished to make stones adored to the detriment of the true God. If the magicians make phantoms appear, if they evoke the souls of the dead, if they make children, goats, tables utter oracles; if they imitate miracles like able charlatans; if they even know how to send dreams by the intermediary of angels and demons whom they have invoked, all the more would these seducing powers do, for themselves, what they undertake for alien interests.'

Tertullian, we see, is convinced that such and such a vestal, accused of infidelity to her vow, has proved her innocence by carrying water in a sieve, and that such another has given the same proof by drawing a vessel with her girdle, that children, goats and tables, obeying the injunction of certain men, have predicted the future. But he explains that these facts, and others of the same kind, which are superior to human powers, are produced by the demons, with the aid of human collaborators; he believes in magic.

Origen has the same belief, as is proved by his dissertation upon the Magi who came to adore Jesus at Bethlehem (*Contra Celsum*, 1, 60). According to him, these personages were in touch with demons, whose co-operation permitted them to accomplish wonders. Now, one day, this precious co-operation failed them. They concluded that the activity of the demons had been checked by a superior power. And as, just at this moment, a star shone in the sky, the Magi, who knew the prophecy of Balaam contained in *Numbers* xxiv. 17, understood that the child foretold by the star had been born. Therefore they set out and followed the star. Here is the essential passage of his dissertation :

'I shall say to the Greeks, that the Magi who had commerce with the demons, and who evoked them according to the rules of their art, in order to do what they pleased, succeeded in their desires so long as no influence, divine and superior to that of the demons, intervened to paralyse their efforts.'

Saint Augustine's opinion about magic is contained in the following texts from the *City of God:*

'10, 9 : The miracles (of Moses) . . . were worked by the simplicity of faith and not by the spells, the sacrilegious receipts of a criminal curiosity called magic, goety, or theurgy. A difference is alleged between these practices ; those whom the vulgar call sorcerers, and who give themselves up to goety, are willingly abandoned to the punishment of the laws, while those who practise theurgy are eulogised. But both are in servitude to the deceiving rites of the demons, called by the name of angels.

'10, 16 : All the miracles of paganism mentioned by history . . . I mean the miracles where the intervention of the power of the demons is obvious : the images of the household gods brought from Troy by Æneas and moving by their own power from one place to another; the stone that Tarquin cut with his razor; the serpent of Epidorus, which followed Æsculapius faithfully to Rome; the ship bearing the idol of the great Phrygian goddess, which resisted the united efforts of men and oxen, and which, when attached to the girdle of a woman, began to move, to testify to her chastity; the vestal, accused of defilement, justifying herself by the proof of a sieve, wherein remained the water she drew from the Tiber; these wonders and a host of others, are they comparable in might to those of which God's people were witness?

'21, 6: Let us add the magic miracles of men acting by the power of demons and the magic miracles of demons acting by themselves; miracles which we cannot deny without contradicting the Holy Scriptures. . . . There are numerous deeds accomplished by the demons: deeds which we ought to avoid with all the more care because their wondrous character is undeniable.'

Augustine thinks that the demons produce here below deeds which surpass human power. He thinks that, in the exercise of their activity, these evil spirits utilise, not always, but often, the co-operation of men, to whom they communicate their powers. Thus he believes in magic.

Saint Cæsarius of Arles (*Sermon* 278 in the *Appendix to the Sermons of Saint Augustine*) forbids, under the gravest penalty, the faithful from consulting sorcerers. It was pointed out to him that the indications provided by these individuals are often the only way of escaping from the greatest dangers. He answers :

> ' I agree, my dear brothers, God, as I have already told you, permits the Devil to do this in order to try the Christians.'

Thus Cæsarius believes that the sorcerers are the depositories of the might of the Devil. It is unnecessary to prolong our inquiry further. There have been, in all times, in the Church, men called magicians, sorcerers and other analogous names, who received from Satan certain supernatural powers. The existence of these agents of the Devil is attested by the Fathers, whose most important testimony has just been cited; and then by the Doctors of the Middle Ages who, if we questioned them, would give us the same reply. Now we must discover the functions or, if you like, the occupations of the sorcerers.

Chapter XXIV

SORCERERS AND WITCHES:
THEIR FUNCTIONS

FOR several centuries the sorcerers occupied themselves almost exclusively in revealing the future or in indicating to mankind, above all to the sick, useful recipes. As the preachers explained it, the Devil used the doing of good as a bait to attract the Christians into his net and, little by little, separate them from the Church. But, later, the enemy of the human race, without renouncing any of these philanthropic actions, which still served his interests, accorded to the sorcerers several other powers that are frankly evil, notably: power to put Christians into a state of demoniac possession, to organise the Sabbath, and to produce storms and tempests.

§ I. THEY PRODUCED DEMONIAC POSSESSIONS

I have already spoken of demoniac possessions, and I have presented them as the exclusive work of Satan. That was true until towards the beginning of the fifteenth century. But, after that date, Satan often gave full power to the sorcerers to carry out this task.

It was the Devil who, by himself or by his sub-ordinate demons, took up residence in the bodies of the demoniacs; but it was the sorcerers who chose the victims and sent them their invisible guests. They accomplished this infamous ministry silently, and without revealing themselves.

How, then, were they known? By the denunciations of their victims. There were many demoniacs who pointed out the sorcerers whose maleficent influence they had suffered. Here are a few examples.

In 1609, in a convent at Aix, two nuns were possessed, the first by a legion of demons, the second by three demons, one of whom was called *Verrine*. One day *Verrine* denounced the priest Gaufridi as the prince of magicians and, shortly afterwards, the first demoniac also began to speak, and accused the same Gaufridi of having ravished her virginity in a cave, in the presence of the worshippers of Beelzebub. Gaufridi enjoyed universal esteem but, from the day the demons made him known as a sorcerer, not an atom of doubt was possible as to his culpability. We shall see later the consequences of this affair.

Some years later, in 1613, several nuns of the convent of Saint Bridget at Lille were tormented by the demon. One day three of them declared that the Devil had been introduced into the convent by the Sister Marie de Sains. The accused had until then passed for a saint: instantly she was looked on as a witch.

And now we come to the Ursulines of Loudun who, in 1632, were tormented by the demon, and of whom we have already spoken. These nuns said that the evil was caused by Urbain Grandier, curé of Saint Peter of Loudun. Urbain Grandier, far from being a saint, led a dissipated enough life, and every one at Loudun knew it. But he had had no relations with the Ursulines. So, when he heard of the denunciation that had been made about him, he protested and complained to the authorities. We shall see that his protest was useless.

§ 2. THEY TOOK PART IN THE WITCHES' SABBATH

The Witches' Sabbath was a nocturnal assembly of men and women. They went to it voyaging through the air, having for steed either a broomstick, or a demon disguised as a dog, or some other analogous vehicle. Their object was the worship of Satan; after which men and women gave themselves up to debauchery. The 'Witches' Sabbath' (the thing, but not the name, which is later) is first mentioned in the book *De ecclesiasticis disciplinis*, 2, 364, by Reginon, a monk of the tenth century. And his text, used by Burchard, then by Yves de Chartres, then by Gratian (the latter inserted it in his famous *Decretum*, 2, 26, 5, 12), became part of the canonical legislation. It is the canon *Episcopi*: it was said to be the work of a Council of Ancyra, which never existed. Here is this important ordinance:

' The bishops and their auxiliaries shall work as much as they can to extirpate from their parishes sorcery and magic, which are pernicious inventions of the Devil. They shall cast out ignominiously from their parishes the men and women whom they find addicted to this vice. . . . Holy Church must be purged of this plague. Nor must this be omitted : certain women, perverted and attached to Satan, seduced by the prestiges and phantasmagoria of the demons, believe and profess that at night they ride with Diana, goddess of the pagans, and Herodias, upon the back of certain beasts, in company with an innumerable multitude of women, travelling over immense spaces, obeying the orders of Diana, as a mistress who summons them on certain nights.

'If they were even the only ones to perish in their impiety ! But there are many whom they lure to them. Considerable multitudes, deceived by this false persuasion, believe all these lies, and thus fall back into the pagan errors. The priests must therefore preach everywhere that they know the falsity of these errors, and that these marvels are produced by the evil spirit who seduces the imagination by vain images. It is Satan who . . . after seizing on the soul of an unhappy woman . . . takes on the appearance of diverse persons and deceives the mind which he holds in his power, sometimes by revealing persons unknown, sometimes by serving as guide in strange voyages. And the soul which has abandoned itself to him believes that it has accomplished in its body the things which are passing solely within itself. Does it not happen to all of us, in dreams, to be led far off and to see during sleep things that we have never seen in the waking state? But no one is foolish enough to believe that these scenes, which unrolled in the mind alone, took place in the body. . . . Therefore it must be proclaimed loudly that those who believe these things have lost the faith, and that they no longer belong to God, but to him in whom they believe, that is to say, to the Devil.'

In this text there is a statement and a judgement. Certain women allege that they voyage through the air at night under the guidance of supernatural beings: that is the statement. And here is the judgement: first, these supernatural beings can only be the goddess of the pagans, Diana, and Herodias, of whom the Gospels speak. Secondly, these alleged voyages do not exist, and never have existed. Without doubt, magic, the pernicious invention of the Devil, is a reality: and the unhappy women who affirm that they voyage during the night are seduced by the Devil. But this evil spirit confines himself to acting upon their imagination. The travels through the air are dreams, dreams differing in no wise from ordinary dreams, save for their cause, which is the Devil. Thirdly, those who believe in the travels through the air belong to the Devil, they no longer belong to God. Let us remember that the canon *Episcopi*, derived from Reginon through the intermediary of Burchard and of Yves, represents the thought of the ecclesiastical legislation of the tenth, eleventh and twelfth centuries; and let us conclude that the Church at this period, while recognising the diabolic origin of the Witches' Sabbath, denied its reality.

But the women who took part in the nocturnal assemblies of the Sabbath opposed their personal experience to the negations of the canonists and the theologians. And the faithful, witnesses of the absolute conviction of the witches, took their side. While the theologians said: 'The Witches' Sabbath is nothing but a diabolic illusion,' the people retorted: 'The Witches' Sabbath is a reality': there was conflict between the theologians and the people.

Conflicts of this kind, which were not rare, usually ended in the victory of the people. It was so in this case: the people refused to abandon its position, but the theologians did not capitulate at once. The doctors long persevered in their denials. At the end of the twelfth century, John of Salisbury, Bishop of Chartres, in his *Polycraticus* (2, 17, end), spoke of the Witches' Sabbath in the same terms as those of the canon *Episcopi*. And, at the beginning of the fourteenth century, the Council of Treves used the same terms in its canon 81. But this obstinacy could not be indefinitely prolonged. In the course of the thirteenth and fourteenth centuries, the Devil was pursued by the Church with a zeal and an activity that had never been equalled. Now, the more his influence was combated, the more it developed. Sorcerers and witches accomplished in his name and with powers received from him wonders ever more prodigious. Their predictions came true, their pretensions were fulfilled. Why could they not have voyaged through the air at night, they who could do everything? And

THE MARK OF THE DEVIL'S CLAWS

SATAN REBAPTISING THE SORCERERS

why should they, whose assertions were in every-thing else well founded, have lied when they related their aerial voyages to meet Satan?

The theologians at last understood that their atti-tude was illogical, and they abandoned it. Already, at the end of the twelfth century, Alain of Lille, in his book *Against the Heretics*, I, 63, relates, as a thing not absolutely certain but probable, that the ' Cathares ' adored Lucifer, who appeared to them in the shape of a cat. In 1231 Pope Gregory IX denounced, with terror, the nocturnal assemblies which took place in Germany, and in which the Devil appeared in the shape of a toad, a white phantom, and a black cat. It was a progression towards the Sabbath. A little later, Albertus Magnus, in the course of an argument entered into on this subject before the bishop of Paris, cited the case of the daughter of the count of Schwa-lenberg, who was carried off every night for several hours. This time the Sabbath itself made its entry into theology, and was introduced into it by one of the greatest doctors, and there it remained. Apart from a few exceptions, among which is the text of the Council of Treves of 1310 mentioned above, the theologians taught that the Witches' Sabbath was a reality. And, besides, the facts gave their conclusion a supplementary certainty.

At this period when, as we shall see, the legislation against sorcery reached an unheard-of degree of fero-city, many sorcerers were burnt for having taken part in the Sabbath, and this torment was inflicted upon them by the Pope's own order. Now these wretches would have been unjustly condemned for participa-

N

tion in the Sabbath if this participation had been imaginary. And, on the other hand, the Church was incapable of punishing wrongly. Therefore, the Witches' Sabbath belonged to the domain of reality. This argument appeared invincible to the Inquisitor, Bernard of Como, who inserted it triumphantly in his book *Lucerna Inquisitorum*, p. 144.

§ 3. THEY PRODUCED STORMS AND TEMPESTS

The belief in the influence of man over the loosing of the plagues of Nature goes back, as we know, to the earliest ages of humankind. In the ninth century, the archbishop of Lyons, Agobard, showed the faithful that this belief did wrong to God, who has reserved to Himself the government of the world, and, further, that it was extravagant.[1] Two centuries later, Pope Gregory VII, writing to the King of Denmark, said to him, in substance: 'I learn that, in your country, the priests are held responsible for the plagues of nature, for epidemic diseases and for the accidents which happen to people. I learn, moreover, that women also are accused of causing all these evils and, for this reason, are persecuted. Put an end to these abominable extravagances, under pain of seeing the anger of God fall upon your people.'[2] At the same epoch, the priest, in the confessional, subjected the

[1] *Contra insulsam vulgi opinionem de grandine et tonitruis*, Migne, 104, 147.
[2] *Registrum*, 7, 21, Migne, 148, 564.

penitent to a long interrogatory, which we know through Burchard, in which we note the following question (68) : [1]

> 'Did you believe those who pretended to be able, by their incantations to the demons, to raise up storms or change the inner feelings of men ? Have you yourself given yourself up to these abominable practices ? If you have believed in or carried out this practice, you will do a year of penance.'

As we see, what the Church forbade Christians to do, during the early Middle Ages, was not only to have recourse to demons to raise up storms, but also to believe in this practice, to attribute to it any reality whatsoever. The question inscribed in Burchard's manual is found again in the manuals of confession of the fourteenth and even of the fifteenth century, which proves that the Church long continued to forbid belief in the intervention of sorcerers in the plagues of Nature. But the sorcerers continued, they too, to raise up tempests and to produce other analogous catastrophes, with the help of the Devil. In the end, they were taken seriously. About 1431 the Dominican Nider explained in his *Formicarius* how the sorcerers went about to raise storms, make hail fall, transport to their own places the harvests of their neighbours, and make women sterile. Nider was one of the lights of the Council of Bâle : he had his information from the judge at Berne, who had it from the sorcerers themselves, who had previously been subjected to torture. Thus no doubt could be raised

---

[1] Schmitz, *Die Bussbuchern*, 2, 425.

against the well-foundedness of his assertions. The *Formicarius* became authoritative. In 1481 the Augustinian monk Hollen, writing the *Præceptorium*, related in it the history of a woman of Norway who sold wind in a sack closed by a cord with three knots. A gentle wind rose when the first knot was undone; the wind became violent after the disappearance of the second knot: finally, a furious tempest arose when the third knot was untied.[1] And, in the *Malleus Maleficarum*, published in 1486, the Dominican Sprenger tells us (2, 1, 15) that, to produce hail, the sorcerers make a hole, pour water into it, and stir it with their fingers. The *Malleus Maleficarum*, which was, in some sort, under the patronage of Innocent VIII, was the manual of the inquisitors. From the end of the fifteenth century on, the sorcerers—or, rather, the witches—for it was above all a question of women—shouldered the responsibility for the catastrophes that happened in Nature.

[1] Jannsen, 8, 525.

PART FIVE

The War of the Church against the Devil

Satan torments mankind. He torments men sometimes himself, by lodging in their bodies in such a way as to make them ' possessed ' ; sometimes by the intermediary of sorcerers, who are his agents, or by the intermediary of certain creatures of Nature. The Church defends mankind ; and her defence, based on methods of aggression, takes two principal forms, which are : exorcism and chastisement. The Church exorcises men to chase from their bodies the Devil who has taken up residence in them. She also exorcises those creatures of Nature whom the Devil uses to torment mankind. As for the sorcerers, she chastises them and, formerly, she handed them over to the secular arm. She only warred upon them in order to protect mankind from their maleficence. Thus her struggle against the Devil, under the multiple forms which it takes, is always a ministry of defence and of protection for mankind. Let us see her at work in the exercise of this ministry.

Chapter XXV

EXORCISM OF THE CREATURES OF NATURE

§ 1. EXORCISM FOR THE BLESSING OF WATER

SALT and water are exorcised every Sunday in all the parishes of the Catholic universe. For this reason : Before beginning High Mass, the priest goes over all the church and sprinkles the faithful with holy water. Besides, all Catholic churches and chapels are provided with fonts, from which the congregation as they enter take with their fingers a few drops of holy water. Moreover, devout people have in their homes holy water with which, morning and evening, they make the sign of the cross. Finally, at Catholic burials, the mourners throw holy water upon the coffin with an aspersorium. These examples, to which others could be added, show the rôle of holy water in the Catholic liturgy. Now holy water is water which has received a blessing, and into which there have been thrown a few pinches of blessed salt. The water is blessed ; the salt which is thrown into it is also blessed. But both, before being blessed, have received a preliminary exorcism. The salt is exorcised first ; then comes the turn of the water. Such is the ceremony which is celebrated, every

199

Sunday, in all the sacristies a few minutes before High Mass.

The formula for the exorcism of salt is the following :

'I exorcise thee, O creature of salt, by the living ✠ God, by the true ✠ God, by the holy ✠ God ; by that God who, by the prophet Eliseus, commanded thee to be cast into the water, to cure its barrenness : that thou mayest by this exorcism be made beneficial to the faithful, and become to all of those who make use of thee, healthful both to soul and body : and that in what place soever thou shalt be sprinkled, all illusions and wickedness and crafty wiles of Satan may be chased away and depart from that place ; and every unclean spirit commanded in his name, who is to come to judge the living and the dead and the world by fire.'

And this is the formula for the exorcism of the water, which, as we shall see, closely resembles the foregoing :

'I exorcise thee, O creature of water, in the name of God ✠ the Father Almighty, and in the name of Jesus Christ ✠ His Son, our Lord, and in the virtue of the Holy ✠ Ghost: that thou mayest, by this exorcism, have power to chase away all the power of the enemy; that thou mayest be enabled to cast him out, and put him to flight with all his apostate angels, by the virtue of the same Jesus Christ our Lord, who is to come to judge the living and the dead and the world by fire.'[1]

[1] Ord. adm., Tit. XI, Cap. 1.

Once exorcised, that is to say, delivered from the demons lodged in them, the salt and water are able to receive the divine benediction. And water once blessed has the virtue of exorcising, of delivering from the Devil and his subordinates all those places on which it is scattered. This is what the prayers that we have just read mean, and also the following prayer, which closes the liturgy of benediction and in which the Church, which is always exorcised, says to God:

'Regard with a favourable countenance this creature of salt and water, enlighten it with thy bounty, sanctify it with the dew of thy fatherly goodness, that wheresoever it shall be sprinkled all infestation of the unclean spirit may depart and all fear of the venomous serpent may be chased away, through the invocation of thy holy name...'

Saint Augustine mentions the following exorcism, carried out in his diocese, and almost under his eyes (*City of God*, 22, 8, 6):

'The former tribune Hesperius dwells in our country. He possesses in the territory of Fussales a property which bears the name of Zubeda. Seeing that his animals and his slaves were the victims of an epidemic, and perceiving that his house was the prey of evil spirits, he, during my absence, besought our priests to send one of them to chase out these maleficent beings by his prayers. A priest went; he offered the sacrifice of the body of Christ and prayed so much that he was able to obtain a cessation of the plague. By the mercy of God, the evil was instantly stopped.'

§ 2. THE EXCOMMUNICATION OF VERMIN

The excommunication and malediction of vermin, which was customary in the Middle Ages, is allied to the exorcism of the creatures of Nature. These two operations depended upon the principle that vermin served as the instrument of Satan. The author of the *First Life* of Saint Bernard tells us (1, 52) that this man of God, being in a place infested with flies (Foigny, near Laon), cried: 'I excommunicate them.' Immediately, the flies passed from life to death, and were removed by the shovelful. Here is a letter which the clergy of Langres received, in 1552, from the vicar-general :[1]

'By the authority of the reverend father in God, Monseigneur Claude of Langres, by the grace of God Cardinal priest of the Holy Roman Church, in the name of Givry, bishop, duke of Langres and peer of France, I, his vicar-general in matters spiritual and temporal, by the authority of the Holy and Indivisible Trinity, trusting in the divine mercy and full of pity, I summon, in virtue of the Holy Cross, armed with the buckler of faith, I command and I conjure, a first, a second and a third time, all the flies vulgarly called *urebires*, and all the other beasts hurtful to the fruit of the vine, that they cease immediately from ravaging, from gnawing, from destroying and pillaging the branches, the buds and the fruit ; never to have

[1] *Bulletin de la Société d'Histoire naturelle de la Haute-Marne*, 1912, p. 19.

this power in the future; to retire into the most distant places in the forests, so that they can no more harm the vines of the faithful, and to go forth from the land. And if, *by the counsels of Satan,* they obey not this ordinance and continue their ravages, in the name of the Lord God and in virtue of the powers aforementioned, by the Church, I curse and hurl the sentence of malediction and anathema upon these *urebire* flies and their posterity.'

It is unnecessary to say that the malediction was the pain of death.

CHAPTER XXVI

BAPTISMAL EXORCISM

THE 'possessed' or demoniacs who alone have until now attracted our attention, are not, in truth, the only victims of the Devil. All men, as a result of the fall of Adam are, when they enter the world, in the power of the infernal spirit. Thus all need to be exorcised. This is what takes place in Baptism. That which constitutes the sacrament, properly speaking, of baptism, is the infusion of water upon the forehead of the child, accompanied by a formula which the minister recites. It is this rite which procures Christian life. But before becoming a Son of God, the unhappy son of Adam is torn from the empire of the Devil. Thus there are two kinds of exorcism provided for men, that which takes place at baptism and that which is received by demoniacs.

Three exorcisms precede the administration of baptism proper. The first takes place at the beginning of the ceremony. It comprises a gesture and a formula. The priest breathes three times upon the face of the child.

The second follows the ritual of the salt. When the priest has put a grain of exorcised salt in the child's mouth, he recites a prayer, then addressing himself to the Devil, he says to him:

'Exorcizo te immunde spiritus, in nomine

Patris ✠, et in Filii ✠, et in Spiritus Sancti ✠, ut exeas, et recedas ab hoc famulo Dei *N*.: Ipse enim tibi imperat, maledicte damnate, qui super mare ambulavit et Petro mergenti dexteram porrexit. Ergo, maledicte diabole, recognosce sententiam tuam et da honorem Deo vivo et vero, da honorem Jesu Christo Filio ejus, et Spiritui Sancti, et recede ab hoc famulo Dei *N*. quia istum sibi Deus et Dominus noster Jesus Christus ad suam sanctam gratiam et benedictionem, fontemque Baptismatis vocare dignatus est.'

These two first exorcisms are carried out at the door of the church.

The third takes place when the child has reached the baptismal font. It begins with this formula:

'Exoriczo te, omnis spiritus immunde, in nomine Dei Patris omnipotentis ✠, et in nomine Jesu Christi ✠, Filii ejus Domini et Judicis nostri et in virtute Spiritus ✠ Sancti, ut discedas ab hoc plasmate Dei *N*. quod Dominus noster ad templum sanctum suum vocare dignatus est ut fiat templum Dei vivi et Spiritus Sanctus habitet in eo. Per eumdem Christum Dominum nostrum, qui venturus est judicare vivos et mortuos et sæculum per ignem.'

After which the priest wets with his saliva the ears of the child, saying: 'Ephatha, that is to say, Be opened'; then his nostrils, pronouncing these words: 'For the odour of sweetness.' Finally he adds:

'Tu, autem, effugare, diabole: approquinquabit enim judicium Dei.'

When he has been duly exorcised, the child is baptised with water which has been exorcised on Holy Saturday or Whit Saturday. Nowadays it is often held sufficient to ' sprinkle ' the new-born, that is, to procure them the essential part of the sacrament of baptism, and the supplementary ceremonies are deferred until more favourable circumstances. When the child receives these complementary rites, he has been, for a longer or a shorter time, baptised. Thus, by definition, he is the child of God and he escapes from the empire of the Devil. The exorcisms, therefore, no longer have any sense. But the Church, who watches with jealous care over the least parts of her liturgy, is no whit embarrassed by so small a matter. She exorcises the child and thrice chases from its body the Devil who, according to the principles of the faith, is not there. And, besides, Saint Thomas, in his *Summa*, 3, 71, 2 and 3, sets forth certain most learned considerations which go to justify this discipline.

Chapter XXVII

EXORCISMS UPON DEMONIACS

FIRST let us examine the New Testament. We have seen that, during his sojourn at Philippi (*Acts* xvi. 17), St Paul was pursued by a girl tormented by a spirit of divination. Now let us complete the account in the *Acts:*

> 'But Paul, being sore troubled, turned and said to the spirit, I charge thee in the name of Jesus Christ to come out of her. And it came out that very hour.'

The sojourn of the Apostle at Ephesus was marked by analogous deeds, which *Acts* xix. 12 mentions briefly in these terms :

> 'Unto the sick were carried away from his body handkerchiefs or aprons, and the diseases departed from them, and *the evil spirits went out.*'

It is true that several Jewish exorcists tried to compete with Paul. But they achieved nothing but a lamentable failure, as is proved by the following text from the *Acts* xix. 14 :

> 'And the evil spirit answered and said unto them, Jesus I know, and Paul I know; but who are ye? And the man in whom the evil spirit was leaped on them, and mastered both of them, and

207

prevailed against them so that they fled out of that house naked and wounded.'

Paul therefore cast out demons at a period when the demons were the souls of the dead, and his success placed him above all the other exorcists who were outside the Christian movement. In any case, the magicians of Ephesus recognised the superiority of the Apostle of Christ, as is witnessed by this text from *Acts* xix. 19 :

> 'And not a few of them that practised curious arts brought their books together, and burned them in the sight of all : and they counted the price of them, and found it fifty thousand pieces of silver.'

Paul eclipsed the Jewish and pagan exorcists. But was he the only one within the Christian movement to cast out demons ? The answer to this question is provided by the *Acts* and, above all, by the Synoptic Gospels.

The *Acts*, one of whose objects is to establish the superiority of Peter over Paul, tell us (v. 16) that Peter's shadow, by itself, was sufficient to cure the sick and 'them that were vexed with unclean spirits.' The Synoptic Gospels show us that the first disciples were invested by Christ with the power of chasing out demons, and that they exercised this power. Here it is sufficient to quote the following texts :

> *St Mark* vi. 6: 'And he went round about the villages, teaching. And he called unto him the twelve, and began to send them forth by two and two ; and he gave them authority over the unclean

SATAN GIVES A BOOK OF BLACK MAGIC TO HIS
DISCIPLES IN EXCHANGE FOR A BIBLE

THE RITUAL KISS OF THE BLACK SABBATH

spirits. . . . And they went out and preached that men should repent. And they cast out many demons and anointed with oil many that were sick, and healed them.'

St Luke ix. 1: 'And he called the twelve together, and gave them power and authority over all demons. . . . (x. 17): And the seventy returned with joy, saying, Lord, even the devils are subject unto us in thy name.'

St Matthew x. 1 : 'And he called unto him his twelve disciples, and gave them authority over unclean spirits, to cast them out. . . . (He said to them) Heal the sick . . . cast out demons.'

Now let us consult the Fathers :

According to Saint Justin the prophecies contained in the Old Testament are the principal proof of the divinity of the Christian religion. After the prophecies come the exorcisms carried out by the Christians. Justin proclaims with pride the dominion which his co-religionists possess over the demons. He says (2 *Apol.*, 6, 5) :

' The Christ became man . . . for the ruin of the demons. What is passing before your eyes tells you that. In the world and in your town there are many demoniacs. Now there are many who, among us Christians, have, by adjurations made in the name of Jesus Christ, who was crucified under Pontius Pilate, healed and still heal these demoniacs by chasing from them the demons who possessed them, while the other exorcists and healers remained impotent.'

o

He returns to this subject several times in the *Dialogues*, as is proved by the following texts :

' 30, 3 : We call Jesus Christ Saviour and Redeemer because the force of his name alone makes the demons tremble. Exorcised in the name of Jesus Christ, who was crucified under Pontius Pilate, procurator of Judæa, they are vanquished, so that it is manifest that his Father has given him the power to subject the demons by his name and by his Passion.

' 76, 6 : We who believe in Jesus Christ, Our Lord, crucified under Pontius Pilate, we exorcise all the demons and evil spirits, and they are subject to us.

' 85, 2 : Every demon exorcised in the name of this Son of God, the eldest of all creatures, born of a virgin, a man subject to the law of suffering, crucified by your people under Pontius Pilate, dead, then resurrected and ascended into heaven, is vanquished and subjugated. But if you, on the contrary, attempted an exorcism in the name of any of your kings, judges, prophets or patriarchs, no matter whom, no demon would be vanquished.'

Saint Irenæus (2, 32, 4) explains that the true disciples of Christ, acting in the name of their Master, do good to men according to the gift which they have received. He adds :

' Some expel demons really and truly, to such an extent that, very often, those who have been delivered from evil spirits believe and enter the Church.'

In his *Apologeticus*, Tertullian shows that the gods of the pagans are demons, and that these demons are subjected to the Christians. He says (23) :

'Make a man known by all to be a demoniac appear before your tribunals. Let a Christian, the first-comer, enjoin the spirit to speak: he will render homage to the truth and will admit he is a demon just as, elsewhere, he would falsely pretend to be a God. Similarly, make those who pass as the interpreters of a God appear before you . . . if, not daring to lie before a Christian, they do not avow themselves to be demons, there and then scatter the blood of this insolent Christian. . . . All this dominion that we have over the demons comes from the name of Christ and from the menace of the punishments with which God will strike them by the intermediary of Christ, the Judge. Fearing Christ in God and God in Christ, they obey the servants of God and of Christ. At our contact, at our breath, the thought and image of the fire which awaits them seizes them. In spite of themselves, a prey to the groaning and confusion you have witnessed, they obey our injunctions and come forth from the bodies. Believe them when they say the truth, you who believe them when they deceive. . . . The avowals of your gods often make Christians, for one cannot believe in them without believing in Christ. . . . (37) (If we went forth from the empire) who would deliver you from these invisible enemies, which ruin your spirits and your bodies ? Who would repulse the demons, whom we chase out freely, without any salary? To avenge ourselves, we would only have to leave you as a prey to these wicked spirits.'

The treatise *De Idolatria* II, shows us that a Christian cannot exercise the trade of an incense-seller without making himself a purveyor of the cult of the idols. It continues :

' When this Christian incense merchant passes in front of the temples, how can he spit upon the smoking altars ? . . . How shall he dare to chase his clients (the demons), for whom his house is a granary of abundance ? But, even if he does chase out the demon, he cannot reassure himself about his faith. It is not an enemy whom he is chasing out.'

We read in the book *Ad Scapulam*, 2 :

' Not only do we hold the demons in horror, we combat them, we pour our contempt upon them, we expel them from the bodies of men, as is known to many. . . . (4) . . . A clerk, who was thrown to earth by a demon, was delivered. Children, persons of good family (I do not occupy myself with the common people), have been healed of demons or of illnesses.'

To Tertullian let us add Minucius Felix, whose *Octavius*, 27, celebrates the exorcisms accomplished by Christians in terms similar to those of the *Apologeticus*, 23.

Origen mentions Christian exorcism, above all, in the book *Contra Celsum*. He says :

' 1, 6 : Celsus, alluding, I think, to those who cast out demons, said, I know not with what motive, that the Christians hold their power from the names of the demons. This allegation is a pure calumny. For the power put forth by the Christians does not come from the invocation of the demons, but from the utterance of the name of Jesus, combined with the commemoration of his life. It is these words which have often made demons come forth from the bodies of men ; above all, when those who pronounce them have a pure conscience and a firm faith.

' 1, 25 : Many a time the name of our Jesus has been seen manifestly to cast out demons from bodies and souls that were possessed by them.

' 1, 46 : Traces of the Spirit which appeared in the form of a dove still remain among the Christians, for they cast out demons and heal divers maladies. . . .

' 7, 4 : (Concerning the spirit which moves the Pythoness when she utters prophecies.) What are we to think of this spirit, save that it is of the same order as those demons from whom Christians, not a few, delivered those who were tormented by them? They obtain this result without recourse to magic or to therapeutic receipts by prayer and by conjurations so simple that the least of mankind is capable of them. Besides, it is generally persons without culture who accomplish this ministry.'

In his letter to Bishop Magnus (69), Cyprian, after having given his advice as to the baptism conferred by heretics, speaks of the baptism administered to the sick lying in their beds. This baptism was suspect to many. Cyprian favours it and defends it against the objections that were being made against it. One of these objections consisted in saying that the sick thus baptised were still agitated by demons at the moment when the baptismal rite was conferred upon them. Cyprian replies (69, 15) :

' The Devil perseveres in displaying his perversity until the salutary water has arrived. But he loses in baptism all the venom of his malice. Thus Pharaoh, obstinately attached to his perfidious projects, was able to resist successfully until he came to the edge of the water ; in that moment he was vanquished and swallowed up. Now the blessed apostle Paul tells us that the sea wherein Pharaoh was swallowed up was the symbol of baptism. He says that everything that then passed was the image of that which takes place in us. It is, indeed, what happens to-day. Flagellated, burnt, tortured by the exorcists who join their human voices to the divine power, the Devil often declares that he will depart and leave in peace the men of God. He is deceiving us and, beneath this lie, he is concealing the obstinacy of Pharaoh of old. But, when the salutary water intervenes, when the sanctification of baptism is conferred, then we must know and believe that the Devil is crushed. . . . The evil spirits can remain no longer in the body of a man who has been baptised and sanctified, and which has become the dwelling of the Holy Ghost.

And besides, this is what experience teaches us. Those who, under the stress of necessity, have received, in a state of sickness, baptism and grace, are delivered from the unclean spirit which formerly agitated them. . . . And, on the other hand, those who have received baptism while well are, if they afterwards sin, tormented anew by the unclean spirit.'

In his book *To Demetrius*, the Bishop of Carthage shows this ferocious adversary of the Christians what are the gods to whom he devotes himself (15) :

' Ah ! if you would only listen to them and see them when, adjured by us, tormented by the spiritual lash of our words, they are expelled from the bodies of which they had taken possession ; when, in the midst of the lamentations and groans torn from them by the rods of human speech joined to the divine power, they confess the judgement that is to come ! Come, and thou wilt see that we speak truth. Since these are thy gods, at least believe in those whom thou honourest. . . . Thou wilt see paralysed and trembling before us those whom thou veneratest and worshippest as thy lords. . . .'

From the fifteenth century onwards, demoniac possessions were more numerous than before. Conformably to the law of supply and demand, exorcists, too, abounded. And, after Luther, the Protestant exorcists in Germany rivalled the Catholic. Each Confession published reports which related the prowess accomplished by its own exorcists. At Spalt, in 1584, a Lutheran preacher made vain attempts to chase the Evil One from the body of a good-wife of the town. The demon mocked him and played him a thousand monkey tricks, and only gave way before a Catholic exorcism. The ' terrifying and most truthful ' gazette, which relates this fact came, it goes without saying, from a Catholic press. Naturally, among the Protestants, it was totally different. In 1606 the preacher Nicholas Blum related the history of a demon who had resisted the efforts of the Catholics and the Calvinists, and had only been vanquished by the Lutherans.[1]

[1] Janssen, 6, 444.

Chapter XXVIII

THE CORPORATION OF EXORCISTS

§ I. ITS EXISTENCE DURING THE FIRST THREE CENTURIES

L ET us return to the first three centuries and survey the information furnished by our texts as to the number of exorcisms in this period, the mode of their administration, their efficacity, and their importance.

If we are to believe Tertullian, demoniacs were very numerous, and the disappearance of the Christians who exorcised these unhappy people would have been, for the Roman Empire, what the disappearance of all its doctors would be to a modern country. That is one of the unmeasured exaggerations which are not rare in the *Apologeticus*. But, when one has set aside the hyperbole of Tertullian, there is still the testimony of Justin, Irenæus, Origen, Cyprian ; and this testimony must be taken into consideration. In the course of the first three centuries, the exorcisms practised by Christians were by no means rare.

By whom were the exorcisms accomplished ? Tertullian has told us that the first-comer among Christians cast out the demons ; and we have heard Origen say that the ministry of exorcism was exercised most often by uncultured persons. And the correspondence of Saint Cyprian gives us a letter (23) addressed to the Bishop of Carthage by the confessor Lucian, who had at his side two members

' of the clergy, an exorcist and a reader.'

Further, the letter of Pope Cornelius to Fabius of Antioch (quoted in part by *Eusebius*, 6, 437) says that the Church of Rome comprises, in the middle of the third century :

' forty-six priests, seven deacons, forty-two acolytes, exorcists, readers and doorkeepers to the number of fifty-two, more than fifteen hundred widows and indigent persons, who are all fed by the grace and philanthropy of the Master.'

According to two of our texts, the practice of exorcism was open to all Christians ; according to the two others, it was reserved to the members of the clergy, that is to say, a closed corporation. These data seem contradictory : let us try to harmonise them.

Every craft requires a minimum of natural disposition, in the absence of which it cannot be practised. The deaf-mute who, after studying law, should present himself as an advocate, would find no client. And the one-armed man who wished to be a blacksmith or a mason, would find no hirers. And thus careers which, theoretically, are open to all, are, in practice, secured by the *élite*. The career of exorcism was in the same class. Theoretically, it was accessible to all Christians. But, to exercise it fruitfully, it was necessary to be capable of intimidating the demons, that is to say, the demoniacs; and this required aplomb, a powerful voice and imperious gestures. Tertullian exaggerates, according to his custom, when he tells us that the first-comer among the Christians cast out the demons. But we can, on the contrary, believe Origen, who tells us that the exorcisms were, above all, performed by uncultured persons. The timid, the refined, failed miserably, and such incapable persons were found, above all, in cultivated circles. In short, the well-frequented exorcists, those who had a large clientele and much work, constituted a closed corporation: closed by means of elimination, since all the incapable were excluded from it by the force of circumstances.

Well known and popular, the exorcists enjoyed great prestige among the faithful: they were a force. In order to hold this force in check, to prevent it from working against them, the bishops bought it. The exorcists received their salary from the budget of the diocesan treasury. They were fed by the community, they were part of the clergy.

At this point it is important to avoid an error. Nowadays—and for long it has been so—the order of exorcists is a step through which the priesthood is reached. The young man who is received as exorcist will later be a subdeacon, then deacon, then priest; he remains in his order only for a short time. In the third century, things were different: then those who were exorcists were so for life. Thus the beadles and the Swiss Guards remain to the end of their lives in their respective situations; none of them dreams of attaining superior rank in the hierarchy. Will it be objected that they are not part of the clergy? Dogma, it is true, leaves them outside Holy Orders. But the liturgy, more liberal or, if you like, more archaic, introduces them into its ceremonies and gives them ecclesiastical vestments; it treats them as clerks. And then, we must remember that, in the third century, widows formed part of the clergy.[1]

If we are to believe Justin, Tertullian and Origen, the exorcisms always achieved their object and the Devil, adjured in the name of Jesus, crucified under Pontius Pilate, never failed to leave the body. Cyprian provides details. According to him, as long as baptism has not been administered, the Devil gives promises, but does not keep them. It is only baptism which compels Satan to make off. This really amounts to saying that the exorcisms accomplished upon pagans are of no effect. Cyprian must be exaggerating. Justin, Origen and Tertullian, who addressed themselves to pagans, would not have celebrated with so much emphasis the power of the Christians over the demons if miraculous cures had never been accomplished in respect of pagan demoniacs. There must

---

[1] There is no rule without exceptions and the exceptions confirm the rule. In the third century we do come across a very few examples of exorcists who are elected deacons or bishops. Such was Saint Romanus, of whom Eusebius speaks in his book *Upon the Martyrs of Palestine*, 2, who was deacon and exorcist at Cæsarea; such was Saint Latinus, Bishop of Brescia, whose epitaph says that, before being bishop, he had been an exorcist twelve years and a priest for fifteen years (*Monumenta Ecclesiæ liturgica*, 1, 2838). *The Apostolic Constitutions*, 8, 26, 2 and 3, say, in substance: 'The exorcist does not receive ordination, for the grace which he possesses has been conferred directly upon him by God, and it is revealed by his works. But, if he is needed for the episcopate, the priesthood or the deaconate, he is to be given ordination.'

be some grains of truth in their assertions. But Cyprian's assertion, it too, cannot be completely false. Let us say that the pagans, tormented by demons and confiding in the good offices of Christian exorcists, were sometimes healed, but not always. Cyprian adds that the Christian is delivered from the Devil by baptism, but that the Devil returns when the Christian, forgetful of his baptism, falls once more into sin. This assertion states a fact and, at the same time, interprets it. The fact stated is that the Devil cast out by baptism is not always definitively expelled, and his temporary expulsion is sometimes followed by a renewed offensive. The interpretation is that the return of the Devil is the punishment for sins committed by the Christian. This interpretation, which is very edifying, is none the less arbitrary: let us neglect it. But the statement cannot have been invented: the exorcisms of baptism sometimes had only a temporary effect.

The Christian exorcists practised their art in the name of 'Jesus, crucified under Pontius Pilate.' They claimed no other rôle than that of instruments in the hands of the heavenly Master. Jesus was the veritable conqueror of the Devil and of his subordinate demons. And since, according to the Fathers, the demons hid themselves under the gods venerated by the pagans, Jesus was the conqueror of the gods! Every exorcism was a new triumph by Him who was crucified on Calvary over the pagan divinities, a new proof of the divinity of Christianity. The exorcisms, as miracles, palpable and always renewable, had a practical, demonstrative force superior to the Resur-

rection of the Christ, which belonged to the past and
which was believed without having been witnessed,
and superior to the prophecies of the Old Testament
relative to the coming of Christ, which required
laborious study. The Jews, who, as much as the
pagans, were affected by the exorcisms, tried to dis-
credit them by placing them to the account of other
demons. Then there was introduced into the Synoptic
Gospels the passage wherein Jesus, accused of casting
out the demons by the prince of demons, Beelzebub,
shows how vain and senseless is this reproach. This
passage, which is mentioned by Irenæus but not by
Justin, proved beyond a doubt that the Christian
exorcists held their powers from God, and not from
the demons.

§ 2. LATER IT EVOLVES AND BECOMES ONE
OF THE DEGREES OF THE HIERARCHY

From the fourth century onwards, the corporation
of the exorcists began to evolve. For this reason,
Christ had come upon earth to overthrow the Devil
and the demons, that is to say, to overthrow the gods
of paganism, who were but demons. The material
proof of this victory over the pagan gods was presented each day by the exorcists, who expelled these
gods from the bodies of the demoniacs. Thus we can
understand without difficulty the enormous prestige
which these individuals enjoyed during the first three
centuries.

During the first three centuries : but not beyond

them. From the fourth century onwards, these stars, which had shone so vividly in the Church, paled, and then, little by little, ended in eclipse. What is the new fact that caused this overthrow of an established position? The conversion of the emperor. The emperor, having become a Christian, protected the Church and made war upon paganism, at first covertly, then violently. Then Christ won against the gods a victory in which the exorcists had no part and beside which all their united prowess was nothing. Attention turned from them to the emperor. Their corporation had no further occupation: it disappeared, and there remained scarcely more than a memory of the exorcists.[1]

Saint Cæsarius of Arles sought, at the beginning of the sixth century, to establish this memory in the liturgy. His attempt first became acclimatised in Gaul; then, little by little, it won over the rest of the Church. Since the time of the Ballerini brothers, there has been, at the end of the works of Saint Leo, certain *Statuta Ecclesiæ antiqua*, among which a ritual for ordination is outlined. The exorcists have taken their place in this ritual, between the acolytes and the readers; they constitute an order in it, a step which leads towards the priesthood. This is the institution of Cæsarius of Arles, an institution which

[1] The Council of Laodicea, which belongs to the end of the fourth century, forbade, in its canon 26, exorcisms by those who have not received ordination. These exorcisms must be understood literally; they do not mean catechetical instruction. Here we see the Church reserving to the bishops, priests, and deacons the monopoly of exorcism. But this legislation does not seem to have taken root in the Greek Church.

was accepted by the Roman Pontificate, and which to-day is still in vigour in the Church. The former corps of exorcists no longer exists; but the young men who are preparing for the priesthood receive from the bishop the power to cast out demons. These exorcists are the shadow of the reality that has disappeared.

We must not suppose that demoniac possessions ceased. There were no longer enough to occupy a corporation; but there were still some, and they were cured. Only, in the absence of professional exorcists, the cures were performed by men renowned for saintliness. From the fourth century onwards, an exorcist was such, not by profession but as necessity arose or, if you like, by supererogation, and the exorcist's diploma was acquired by saintliness.

A catalogue of all the exorcisms accomplished since the fourth century would, even if it were possible, be as irksome as useless. Let us confine ourselves to selecting the most striking cases.

Chapter XXIX

CELEBRATED EXORCISTS

§ 1.   THREE GREAT BISHOPS

Saint Ambrose, according to his biographer, Paulinus (*Vita*, 43), cured many demoniacs by laying his hands upon them and enjoining the unclean spirits to depart. In this way he cured, notably, at Florence (28) the son of the Christian Decens, who was tormented by a demon. Paulinus is not a very reliable historian. His accounts do not, perhaps, correspond to the exact truth, but they present us, in any case, with what their author has succeeded in getting believed.

Saint Martin of Tours, who was a great thaumaturge, also accomplished miraculous exorcisms, of which Sulpicius Severus tells us in his *Dialogues*, 3, 6. Here are a few of his tales :[1]

'Each time that Martin came to the church, the demoniacs who were there howled and trembled, as do criminals when the judge arrives. . . . I have seen, at Martin's approach, a demoniac raised up into the air, and stay there without touching the ground. When Martin was exorcising the demons

[1] For the value of Sulpicius Severus' accounts, see Babut, *St Martin de Tours*.

... the unhappy wretches expressed in divers ways the constraint they had to suffer. Some, their feet in the air, seemed to be suspended from the clouds, and yet their clothing was not disturbed and modesty was not offended. Others avowed their crimes without waiting to be interrogated. They even gave their names. One admitted he was Jupiter, another Mercury. ...'

Saint Augustine: The author of his *Life*, Possidius, says (22):

'When he was a priest and also when he was a bishop, he was asked to pray for demoniacs. He prayed to God, not without shedding tears, and the demons came forth from the men whom they held in their possession.'

§ 2. THE FATHERS OF THE DESERT

In his *Lausiac History*, 18, II, Palladius says of the monk Macarius of Alexandria:

'He cured such a great quantity of demoniacs that it is impossible to enumerate them.'

A little further on (18, 22) we read the story of a child, 'worked on by an evil spirit', whom Macarius cured by laying his hands on him. In the same book (22, 9) Palladius, speaking of Paul the Simple, describes the following exorcism performed by this holy monk:

'After a stay of one year (with Antony) Paul was judged worthy of a grace against demons and

sicknesses. On one occasion among others, there
was brought to Antony a demoniac as terrible as
could possibly be imagined, who had a dominating
spirit, and who cursed heaven. Antony, having
examined him, said to those who had brought him:
" This work is not for me for I have not yet been
judged worthy of a gift against this dominating
order ; but this belongs to Paul." Antony therefore conducted them to Paul and said to him :
" Abbot Paul, cast out the demon from the man,
in order that he may return healed to his occupations." Paul said to him : " Why not you ? "
Antony said : " I have no time ; I have other
work." And, having left him, Antony re-entered
his cell. Then the old man, raising himself up,
uttered an efficacious prayer, and said to the
demoniac : " Father Antony orders thee to go
forth from this man." But the demon cried out
with blasphemy : " I will not come forth, thou
vile old man ! " Then the old man, taking up his
goatskin, struck him on the back, saying : " Father
Antony orders thee to go forth ! " The demon
hurled yet more violent curses at Antony and Paul.
Finally Paul said : " Go forth, or I will go and tell
Christ about it. By Jesus, if thou dost not go forth
instantly, I will go to tell it to Christ and he will
hurt thee sorely." The demon blasphemed anew
and cried out: " I come not forth ! " Then
Paul, angered by the demon, went forth from the
hostel in the very middle of the day. Now in
Egypt the heat is like the Babylonian furnace.
Placing himself against a rock of the mountain,

Paul began to pray and said: " Thou, Jesus Christ, crucified under Pontius Pilate, thou art witness that I will not come down from this rock, that I will neither eat nor drink, if I have to die from it, until I have cast out the spirit from the man and until thou hast delivered him." Now these words were scarce spoken when the demon uttered a cry, saying : " Oh! what might! I am cast out. The simplicity of Paul casts me out. And whither shall I go ? " Instantly, the spirit came forth and was changed into a dragon, seventy-six cubits long, which dragged itself towards the Red Sea, so that the word should be accomplished which says (*Proverbs* 12, 17) : " He that uttereth truth showeth forth righteousness." Such was the miracle accomplished by Paul, whom the whole community of brethren surnamed the Simple.'

§ 3.   SAINT CÆSARIUS OF ARLES

The Life of Saint Cæsarius of Arles, written by his disciples, comprises two books. The second book is devoted to the miracles accomplished by the saint. It is there that the following exorcisms are found.

' 15. Cæsarius, being upon a pastoral journey, saw, one day, a woman come to him in tears, who entreated him to heal her serving-woman. The bishop asked questions, which received the following reply :

' " She has a demon whom the country people

call Diana. Nearly every night she is plentifully battered with blows. Often, too, she is taken by two men to the church. The diabolic scourgings which strike her are invisible, but they make her instantly utter cries which put her in such a state that she cannot reply to the people about her. . . ." Cæsarius laid his hands upon the servant and blessed her. Then he gave her some holy oil, with a command to rub herself with it at night. The girl immediately obtained such complete healing that the demon never returned to her.

' 16. In another parish a child of eight presented himself at the altar at the moment when Cæsarius, who had just preached, was beginning the Mass. Tormented by a very evil spirit, the child was seized with a general trembling and foam came from his mouth. This horrible spectacle terrified the whole congregation. Cæsarius, lifting his eyes to heaven, asked God to heal the child : then he left him, to continue the Mass. Then the priest set the child at his feet. . . . As soon as the child was at Cæsarius' feet, he rose up healed. And from that moment the evil spirit never returned to him. I saw him later, as a subdeacon in that very church.

' 17. Cæsarius was confronted with a girl tormented by a terrible demon of a new species. She could not go out of her house without being immediately assailed by a troop of crows, who tore her face and soiled her head and neck while, trembling and foaming, she rolled on the ground. . . . When Cæsarius saw the torn face of this woman, he said to us in a low voice : " To my knowledge the Devil has never yet given himself to this kind of aggression." Then, in front of the holy altar, he laid his hand on her head and blessed some oil, with which he rubbed her eyes and ears. In the sight of every one the girl went back cured to her home. During the two days we passed there she came to the church and, afterwards, she was never again tormented.'

We see that Cæsarius gave an important place to holy oil in his exorcisms. And, besides, he carried on an active propaganda in favour of holy oil, as a consequence of which he became, without wishing it, one of the authors of extreme unction.

§ 4. SAINT FRANCIS OF ASSISI

This is what we read in *Thomas of Celano:*

'A brother was often afflicted with a horrible infirmity, whose name I do not know, and which some think was an evil spirit. Often he was struck from all about and, horrible spectacle, he turned about and rolled, foaming at the mouth. His limbs would first contract, then stiffen, then bend and twist, then become rigid and hard. When he was thus stretched out and rigid, his feet as high as his head, he was lifted up bodily to his full height and then suddenly let fall to earth. Moved with compassion before this grave infirmity, the saintly Father Francis of Assisi went to him and, after uttering a prayer, made the sign of the cross over him and blessed him. The sick man, having returned to health, never thereafter suffered the slightest attack of his sickness. . . . In the town of Castello, there was a woman possessed by a demon. The very holy Father Francis was in this town and the woman was brought to him at the house in which he lodged. From outside, the woman began to grind her teeth, to squint and to cry out in a wretched voice, according to the fashion of wicked spirits. Many inhabitants of the city of both sexes gathered and implored Saint Francis to help the woman ; for a long time the evil spirit had tormented and troubled her by its piercing cries. The holy Father therefore sent her a Brother who was with him, to find out whether it was a question of a demon, or some womanish deceitfulness. When she saw him, the woman began to mock him, knowing that it was not Saint Francis. The holy Father was within at prayer. When he had finished, he came out. The woman began to tremble and to roll on the ground, being unable to bear his influence. Calling her to him, Saint Francis then said : " In the name of obedience, I order thee, thou unclean spirit, to come forth." And it quitted her and left her, without doing her further injury, indignant enough.'

Saint Francis of Assisi was, therefore, a powerful thaumaturge. But his companion, Brother Juniper, was superior to him, as is proved by the following testimony of the *Fioretti:*

'The demons could not bear the purity, the humility and the innocence of Brother Juniper. For, truly, one who was possessed fled through the streets in an unaccustomed direction and went rapidly by twisting paths to a distance of seven miles. His relatives underwent great fatigue in following him. When they came up with him, they asked him why he had fled in this direction. He replied : " Because that idiotic Juniper was in my path and I cannot bear his look." After an inquiry, the relatives found that Brother Juniper had passed by at the very hour the Devil had indicated. This is why Saint Francis, when those who were possessed were brought to him to be healed, and the Devil would not depart immediately, used to say : " If you do not immediately quit this creature, I shall call Brother Juniper." Then the Devil would depart, for he feared the neighbourhood of Brother Juniper.'

§ 5. SAINT NORBERT

Saint Norbert, in the first years of the twelfth century, preached the Gospel in Germany and the North-East of France. In the course of his peregrinations he encountered a woman possessed, whom he undertook to exorcise (*Acta Sanctorum*, 6th June) :

'At first the Devil mocked him. Not letting himself be discouraged, the man of God enjoined the unclean spirit to depart far from the creature of God. At the end of his resources, the demon cried out : " If you want me to go forth from her, permit me to go into that monk who is over there." Norbert said to the people : " Observe his wickedness. In order to outrage the servant of God, this demon wishes to possess him like a sinner. But do not be disturbed. . . ." Then he threw himself yet more violently upon the evil spirit, who said : " What, then, do you want ? Neither you nor anyone else will make me come forth to-day. The black squadrons, if I merely call them, will come to my aid. Come! Rise up for war! Come! Rise up for war! These columns and vaults will fall upon you." At these words, the people fled. But the priest remained in his place without fear. Then the hand of the possessed woman seized hold of her robe to strangle her. The bystanders made as if to stop her, but Norbert said : " Leave her alone! Let her do according to the will of God." She, disconcerted, instantly withdrew her hands. And now the day was far spent. Norbert ordered that the possessed woman should be put into water to exorcise her. As she was blonde, he feared that that might permit the demon to maintain his power over her. So he had her hair cut. Then the demon raged and cried out : " Stranger from France! Stranger from France! What have I done to you that you do not leave me in peace. May every evil fall upon your head to punish you for tormenting me thus! "

'Night having fallen and Norbert observing sadly that the demon had not yet departed, he ordered that the possessed woman should be taken back to her father. The following morning she was brought again to Mass. . . . Norbert resolved to eat no food until the sick woman was cured and, in fact, passed the rest of the day and night fasting. On the following morning he prepared to say Mass; the girl was again brought, and the people gathered to witness the combat between the priest and the demon. Norbert ordered two men to hold the possessed not far from the altar. When he had come to the Gospels, she was brought to the altar, and several passages were read over her head. The demon still mocked, and when the priest next elevated the Host, it cried out : " See how he holds his little god between his hands !" This made the priest of the Lord tremble, and, gathering up all his strength, he began to attack the demon in his prayers and to torment him. Then the demon cried out through the mouth of the girl : " I burn! I burn!" Then the voice howled : " I die! I die!" Then a third time : " I want to go! I want to go! Send me away! " The two men held the possessed woman strongly. But the demon did not let himself be stopped. He escaped, abandoning the vessel he had possessed and leaving behind him nauseating smells. The girl fell to the ground. She was taken back to her father's house, took nourishment, and soon completely returned to health.'

§ 6. SAINT BERNARD

The monk Ernald, one of the authors of the first *Life of Saint Bernard*, relates (Book II) the miracles accomplished by the puissant abbot during his sojourn in Italy. Among these prodigies are the following exorcisms :

' 10. (Bernard is at Milan.) It was felt certain that he would obtain from the Lord everything that he wished. A woman was brought to him who, to the knowledge of the whole world, had been tormented by the spirit of evil for seven years. He was entreated, in the name of the Lord, to put the demon to flight and to give back her health to this woman. The man of God was deeply troubled by the confidence which the people had in him. His humility dissuaded him from attempting an unaccustomed work . . . but, on the other hand, would he not offend God and extend over the people the veil of doubt as to the divine omnipotence if he disappointed their confidence ? A prey to an internal conflict, he put his enterprise beneath the patronage of the Holy Spirit, and devoted himself to prayer ; then, armed with the virtue of heaven, having with him the spirit of strength, he put Satan to flight, after having addressed him severely ; and he gave back to the woman at the same time health and peace. . . .

' 11. Three days later, the servant of God went to the church of Saint Ambrose, there to celebrate the holy sacraments. . . . During Mass, a little girl was presented to him, who was violently tormented by the Devil: he was entreated to give aid to the unhappy girl, and to remove her from the fury of the Devil. The man of God was moved by the sight of this child, who ground her teeth and uttered sharp cries, which made the people tremble. So great a trial at such a tender age inspired him with compassion. He took the paten of the chalice which he was to use to celebrate the holy sacraments. He spread the wine over his fingers, praying inwardly. Then, confident in the divine power, he applied the life-giving liquid to the child's mouth; he made the medicinal drops penetrate into her body. This infusion acted like a burn on Satan, who could not bear it a single instant. Hurried from within by the antidote of the cross, he made his exit in such haste that he provoked a hideous vomiting. Seeing this cure and the humiliating flight of the Devil, the congregation gave to God the glory which is his due.

' 13. Among the demoniacs there was an aged woman, born in Milan, and formerly enjoying public esteem. She was dragged in the steps of the blessed man of God, up to the church of Saint Ambrose. For several years the Devil had taken up residence in her heart, and her torments were such that she could neither see nor hear nor speak. Her teeth chattered, her tongue came out of her mouth like an elephant's trunk: she looked rather a monster than a woman. Her repulsive face, her threatening look, her fetid breath testified to the hideous sojourn Satan made in her. When the man of God saw her, he perceived that the Devil was soldered to her and that he would not come forth easily from a house wherein he had so long inhabited. Turning towards the people, who were very numerous, he ordered them to pray with fervour; then, standing near the altar with the clergy and the monks, he had the woman brought up, firmly held. She kicked, urged by a diabolic force, for she could not be natural, she kicked the abbot and cursed his followers. Not letting himself be upset by this audacity of the Devil, whom he despised, the abbot addressed to God a sweet and humble prayer, asking him to come to his help. Each time he made the sign of the cross over the sacred Host, he turned toward the woman and combated, like an athlete, the spirit of evil with the same sign. The spirit, on its side, each time that the sign of the cross was directed against it, struggled with greater violence; and its rage against the goad was the involuntary index of its suffering.

' When the dominical oraison was finished, the holy man attacked the enemy more vigorously. After putting the holy body of the Lord on the paten of the chalice, he laid the paten on the head of the woman and uttered these words: " This is thy Judge, O evil spirit, this is the sovereign power. Resist if thou canst. He is there, he who, on the eve of his passion, said that the prince of this world would be cast out. This body is that which was formed from the body of a virgin, that was stretched upon the wood of the cross, that was laid in the grave and, in the sight of the disciples, went up to heaven. Thus, by the terrible might of this Majesty, I order thee, evil spirit, to come forth from His servant and never again to touch her in future."

'Being unable to stay any longer and seeing himself obliged to make off, the demon, at the height of his rage, employed the few moments that remained to him to the infliction of greater torments. As for the Holy Father, returning to the altar, he carried out, according to rite, the division of the Host, then he gave place to the deacon, who communicated it to the people. Instantly the woman completely recovered peace and tranquillity. Thus it was that the flight of the Evil One showed the power and the efficacity of the divine sacraments. . . . The tale of the events at Milan spread throughout Italy the renown of the man of God. Everywhere there spread the news that a great prophet had arisen, a man mighty in works and in words, who, by the invocation of Christ, could heal the sick and expel demons from the bodies of the possessed.

' 23. (Bernard is at Pavia.) There was in this town a demoniac whose torments caused the laughter of some and the compassion of others. He barked in such a manner that those who heard him, without seeing him, thought that he was a dog. The man of God was seized with pity when he saw this unhappy wretch, whose barking resembled that of a dog, which is struck or crushed, and which turns upon its aggressors. When he was brought into the presence of the man of God, the panting demoniac barked with more violence than usual. After apostrophising and expelling the Devil by the virtue of Christ, the man of God commanded the man to speak. He, delivered, entered into the church, took part in the ceremonies, made the sign of the cross, listened to the gospel, prayed and rendered to God those religious duties which are rendered by persons healthy in mind.'

Here is another exorcism, of which we read in the fourth *Life*, 2, 15 :

'At Bar-sur-Aube there were two women tormented by demons. Their relations brought them to Clairvaux to obtain their cure from the man of God. As they approached the abbey, one of the devils, speaking through the mouth of the woman whom he tormented, said to the other : " I must go forth from this woman." The other said : " Why is that necessary ? " The first answered : " I can neither see Bernard nor hear his voice." The second said : " Why ? " The first answered : " When Bernard was in the world, I wanted to tempt him and take his virginity from him. He said to me : 'Get thee behind me, Satan ? I adjure thee by Jesus never to harm me nor to look at me.' Because of that, I must depart." Instantly he came forth from the woman, who was healed. The bystanders praised God, saying : " This man is truly holy and the Holy Spirit dwells in him." At this point the servant of God came to the door. What had just been heard and seen concerning the demons was related to him. Then the man of God said : " I give thee thanks, Lord Jesus Christ, for that thou hast never abandoned me. Thou alone art God, thou alone doest miracles. It is thou who hast created the heaven and the earth and all that is therein. Lord, hear my prayer and let my cry come unto thee." After this prayer, turning towards the other woman, he said to the demon : " Demon, enemy of God, come forth from this woman." At these words, the demon came forth from the woman, who was instantly healed.'

§ 7. FATHER SURIN AND THE OTHER EXORCISTS OF LOUDUN

In the famous matter of the convent of Loudun, several Ursulines were tormented by the demon. But the superior, Jeanne des Anges, must alone have our attention, because the ministers of God charged with expelling Satan busied themselves above all with her. The exorcisms which she underwent are divided into two periods, of which one precedes the death of the curé Urbain Grandier, and the other follows it.

The exorcisms of the first period, 1632–1634, had, as their objective, above all, to find out the cause of the evil, that is to say, to find by what way the Devil had taken possession of the body of Jeanne. However, in the first public exorcism, accomplished in the presence of the bailiff and of several doctors, the

A Devil leaves the Body of a Man Possessed

possessed confined herself to declaring that she served as dwelling-place to the demon Asmodeus and to six other demons. As long as she was replying to the questions of the exorcist, she was a prey to convulsions. Then, at the end of a certain time, the convulsions ceased; Jeanne came back to her natural state, knowing nothing of all that had passed during the crisis. The interrogatory was, by the force of things, suspended. To the questions put in Latin, the replies had been made in Latin. But with two solecisms which surprised the laity and embarrassed the exorcist.

The convulsions having returned, a second public séance took place in the afternoon of the same day. The following dialogue took place (still in Latin):

' Does this come from a magician's pact or from the will of God ? '
' It is not the will of God.'
' What is the magician called ? '
' Urbain.'
' Is it Pope Urban ? '
' Grandier.'
' Of what country is this magician ? '
' Le Mans.'
' Of what diocese ? '
' Of Poitiers.'

Other interrogatories took place; but they do not tell us anything important. Let us pass on to the exorcisms which followed the death of Urban Grandier.

Grandier having disappeared, the evil of which he

Q

was the cause ought to have disappeared, too. Nothing of the kind. Jeanne continued to be the prey of demons. The exorcists had, therefore, to prolong their ministry with her. First the unhappy woman was confided to the care of Father Lactance, a Capucin. Out of seven demons who were lodged in the body of Jeanne, the new exorcist expelled three. It was a magnificent success. Unhappily, the demons revenged themselves by entering into the body of Father Lactance, who, at the end of a few weeks, died a prey to terrible convulsions. This is what we learn from the *Relation de ce qui c'est passé aux exorcisms de Loudun*, p. 22.

Lactance was replaced by Father Surin, a Jesuit of great saintliness. Surin acquitted himself with zeal in the ministry with which he was charged. He multiplied the exorcisms upon Jeanne. For a long time his efforts remained fruitless. One day, however, a prodigious success was obtained. Of the four demons who still dwelt in the body of the possessed, one, Leviathan, made off and a second, Isacaaron, while refusing to depart, consented at least to speak. Surin, who owed his first victory to Saint Joseph, again had recourse to the mighty foster-father of Jesus. Repeated summonses were defied. Speaking of Leviathan, Isacaaron said : ' The chief has departed. . . . Now I am master in my house, I am master.' However, in the end, he, too, went. A third demon, Balaam, had preceded him.

There remained the fourth demon, named Behemoth. Surin prepared to dislodge this last evil-doer and, without doubt, he would have succeeded. But hereupon the vanquished demons took the terrible revenge upon their conqueror of which we have already read. Surin, himself invaded by the evil spirits, had to give up his place to Father Resses. It was this new exorcist, the third since the death of Grandier, who succeeded, after laborious conversations, in casting out Behemoth. This memorable event fell upon the 15th of October 1637. For five years, from all points of the kingdom, all eyes had been turned towards the nuns of Loudun.

During this whole time Richelieu had allowed to the nuns and to the exorcists an annual pension of two thousand livres. The departure of Behemoth was thus a benefit for France.

Chapter XXX

THE INSTRUCTIONS OF THE ROMAN RITUAL

EVEN to this day the Church still authorises her ministers to exorcise demoniacs, and to chase the Devil from their bodies. The legislation upon this subject is found in the Roman Ritual in the chapter *De Exorcisandis Obsessis A Dæmonio*. It comprises the directions to follow and the formulæ to recite. Let us begin with the latter.

They are lengthy, very lengthy, and some may be, or even must be, said several times. We shall soon see why. Here is the schema of the exorcism.

The priest, clothed in the surplice and the violet stole, begins by aspersing with holy water the demoniac who, if he is subject to violent crises, has previously been bound. This done, the priest, kneeling, addresses the following prayer to God:

'Domine sancte, Pater omnipotens, æterne Deus, Pater Domini nostri Jesu Christi, qui illem refugem tyrannum et apostatem gehennæ ignibus depustasti, quique Unigenitum tuum in hunc mundum misisti, ut illum rugientem contereret; velociter attende, accelera, ut eripias hominem ad imaginem et similitudinem tuam creatum, a ruina, et dæmonio meridiano. Da, Domine, terrorem tuum super bestiam, quæ exterminat vineam tuam.

Da fiduciam servis tuis contra nequissimum draconem pugnare fortissime ne contemnat sperantes in te, et ne dicat, sicut in Pharaone, qui jam dixit : " Deum non novi, nec Israel dimitto." Urgeat illum dextera tua potens discedere a famulo tuo *N.* (vel a famula tua *N.*) ✠, ne diutius præsumat captivum tenere, quem tu ad imaginem tuam facere dignatus es, et in Filio tuo redemisti.' (*Tit.* X, cap. 1.)

When this prayer is finished, the priest apostrophises the Devil in these terms :

' Præcipio tibi, quicumque es, spiritus immunde et omnibus sociis tuis hunc Dei famulum obsidentibus : ut per mysteria incarnationis, passionis, resurrectionis et ascencionis Domini nostri Jesu Christi, per missionem Spiritus Sancti et peradventurum ejusdem Domini nostri ad judicium, dicas mihi nomen tuum diem, et horam exitus tui, cum aliquo signo : et ut mihi Dei ministro licet indigno prorsus in omnibus obedias : neque hanc creaturam Dei, vel circumstantes, aut eorum bona ullo modo offendas.'

Then come long extracts from the Gospels, prayers, signs of the cross by the dozen and terrifying apostrophes to the Devil, such as this one, for example :

' Adjuro te, serpens antique, per judicem vivorum et mortuorum, per factorem tuum, per factorem mundi : per eum, qui habet potestatem

mittendi te in gehennam, ut ab hoc famulo Dei *N.*,
qui ad Ecclesiæ sinum recurrit cum metu, et
exercitu furoris tui festinus discedas. . . . Et ne
contemnendum putes dum me peccatorem nimis
esse cognoscis. Imperat tibi Deus ✚. Imperat tibi
majestas Christi ✚. Imperat tibi Deus Pater ✚,
imperat tibi Deus Filius ✚, imperat tibi Deus
Spiritus ✚ Sanctus . . . Exi ergo, transgressor. Exi,
seductor, plene omni dolo et fallacia, virtutis ini-
mice, innocentum persecutor. Da locum, impiis-
sime; da locum, dirissime ; da locum Christo. . . .
Sed quid truculente reniteris? quid temerarie
dectrectas ? '

These curses are interminable. However, they do
have an end. But, when the end is reached, we come
to this note in the Ritual :

' All that precedes may be recommenced, if
there be need, until the possessed is completely
delivered.'

Now let us pass on to the directions or, at least, to
those of them which have some interest for us. We
read in the Ritual :

' The priest must not easily believe in possession,
but he must know the signs which permit one to
discern the possessed from those suffering from
some other sickness. . . . But the signs of the presence of a demon are : speaking several words in
an unknown tongue, or understanding words in
such a tongue ; discovering distant and hidden

things; displaying a strength superior to the natural age or condition; and producing other effects of the same kind, of which, the greater the number, the greater the indications of possession.'

And a little further on :

'If the priest perceives that he is prevailing (over the demons), let him continue for two, three, four hours, and longer if he can, until he has attained the victory.'

We know that the most violently convulsed, after a few hours of convulsion and vociferation, fall into prostration and inertia. The last prescription, which enjoins the priest to prolong the séance and to multiply the signs of the cross for four hours or even longer, if he can, is thus essentially derived from experience. The demoniac will be exhausted at the end of four hours and he will be calm, which signifies, in theological language, that he will be delivered from the demon.

The first prescription establishes, for the discernment of demoniac possession rules theoretically acceptable, but whose practical application requires expert hands. Formulated as it is, it restricts the number of demoniac possessions and also the possibility of error. The Church, when she inscribed it in the Ritual, showed great circumspection. Her sons have inspired themselves with her spirit. In nearly all dioceses it is forbidden to priests to exorcise demoniacs without a written authorisation from the bishop. This prohibition, which is not inscribed in the Ritual, completes and develops the rules which the Ritual has promulgated. To-day exorcisms are extremely rare. The Church still proclaims her power to cast out the Devil from the body of those who are possessed ; but she hesitates to use it.

CHAPTER XXXI

THE SORCERERS WERE AT FIRST EXCOMMUNICATED

THE Church has pity on the demoniacs, who are the victims of Satan. But the sorcerers or magicians give their allegiance to this perverse being and work for him. The Church holds them in horror. This horror has always been present; but the form in which it has been expressed has varied in the course of the centuries. The legislation of the Church against sorcerers has passed through two periods: one of relative clemency, when the sorcerers did not forfeit their lives; the other of inexorable severity, when the sorcerers were burnt.[1]

The first legislation comprised excommunication, imprisonment, or expulsion. The Council of Ancyra of 314 promulgates the following prescription in Canon 24:

'Those who predict the future, who follow the customs of the pagans, who bring magicians into their houses to be instructed by them in magic remedies or to accomplish purifications, shall be subjected to five years' penitence.'

The *Apostolic Constitutions* (2, 62) say to the Christians:

'Flee from divination in all its forms and from

[1] Hinschius, *Kirchenrecht*, 5, 397.

the evocation of the dead ; for it is written in *Numbers* 23, 23 : " there is no enchantment with Jacob." And elsewhere (1 *Kings* 15, 23) " divination is a sin."

' The Council of Agda of 506 says in Canon 42 :

' There are certain of the clergy and of the laity who pursue the science of augury and for alleged religious ends practise divination with the aid of what they call " the lots of the saints." . . . Every clerk and every layman who shall be convicted of giving himself up to this practice or of having profited by them shall be considered as not forming part of the Church.'

The Councils of Vannes, 16 (461), of Orleans, 30 (511), of Auxerre, 4 (578), etc., speak in analogous terms, and it would be wearisome to cite their texts. Let us confine ourselves to quoting the two following Councils of the Carolingian epoch : the Council of Riesbach (800) says in Canon 15 :

' Concerning those who practise divination in its diverse forms, who produce tempests or other maleficence, the Council decides that the archpriest of the diocese where these persons shall be discovered shall subject them to a most stringent interrogatory, to lead them to make avowal. But their lives should be preserved and they should be kept in prison until, under God's inspiration they have promised to reform.'

The Council of Paris (850) prescribes, in Canon 23, that women who practise magic shall be subjected to a very severe penitence.

Now let us question the doctors.

About 410 Saint Augustine wrote his book *De divinatione dæmonum*, whose fundamental idea is this: God permits the demons to give, sometimes, true replies to those who consult them ; but He disapproves of such consultations.

About 850 Pope Leo IV replies to the bishops of England, who have asked him if obscure questions could be decided by lot. He says, in substance, this : ' The Council of Ancyra has forbidden to Christians divination and magic. Now, the lots to which you have recourse in your judgements are nothing less than the practice of divination and magic, forbidden by this Council. That is why we wish that the practice of lots be condemned, that there shall never be any question of it among Christians, and that it shall be forbidden on pain of anathema.'

In the thirteenth century Saint Thomas teaches, in the *Summa*, 2, 2, 95, that the Devil, even if he is not expressly invoked, intervenes in one way or another in the diverse forms of divination ; and he bases himself upon the Decretal of Leo IV (he borrows from the *Decree* of Gratian) to condemn the use of lots (95, 8).

Let us add to these texts the Canon *Episcopi* cited previously. It prescribes to bishops that they shall chase out of their dioceses magicians and sorcerers. To sum up, excommunication, imprisonment until conversion, sometimes expulsion from the diocese, such is the fate of sorcerers during the whole of the early Middle Ages, and even in the thirteenth century. This treatment which they had to undergo seems to us severe. It was nothing beside that which awaited them, and of which it now remains to speak.

Before proceeding further let us describe in a word the characteristics of sorcery during this first period. Its principal object was divination, that is to say, the prediction of the future. Its other manifestations were exceptional, which comes to saying that there were few wizards or witches who produced tempests or flew through the air at night, etc. Rarer still, if indeed there were any then, were the authors of demoniac possessions. As for incubi and sucubi, they only existed in a sporadic state, and the persons with whom they slaked their passions were their victims, that is to say, demoniacs, rather than their accomplices, that is to say, sorcerers or witches.

Finally, let us note that the supervision of sorcerers was exercised by the bishops who, as much as possible, shut their eyes in order to see nothing. If they were obliged to take action, they contented themselves with excommunication or with expulsion from the diocese. The pain of imprisonment prescribed by the law was perhaps never applied. We may say that trials for sorcery did not exist. But now we have come to the second period. Things are going to change.

Chapter XXXII

LATER THEY WERE BURNT

IN the twelfth century persons guilty of heresy were often burnt. But this practice, which was carried out by, or at the instigation of, the common people, had no juridical character. In the thirteenth century a Pope arose, who consecrated and inscribed in the Canon Law the custom which had issued from the passions of the vulgar. This Pope was Gregory IX, whose Constitution is dated 1231. From this time on the heretics, after their condemnation, were abandoned to the secular arm, which sent them to the stake.

From the thirteenth century sorcerers were often treated as heretics and sent to the stake. This zeal was not in conformity with the law, for the legislation of Gregory IX struck only at heretics. But it pleased the fanaticism of the people. It was soon to triumph. Little by little the theologians arrived at the conclusion that the practices of sorcery were dictated by heresy, and that the sorcerers erred against the faith. The Papacy gave way. Its capitulation was accomplished in two stages. In 1257 Alexander IV made a first concession in the Bull *Quod super nonnullis*, which authorised the inquisitors to punish sorcerers when their practices were tainted with heresy. By

253

this decision the sorcerers, in many cases, were condemned to be burnt as guilty of heresy ; but sorcery
in itself remained distinct from heresy and escaped
the stake. It was at this period that there lived the
famous Petrus of Abano, who taught medicine at
Padua and devoted himself to alchemy. Petrus,
having been denounced to the Inquisition as a
magician, and accused of being in league with the
Devil, died before the termination of his trial. If he
had not died this opportune death, he would infallibly
have been condemned to the stake, for his corpse was
exhumed and burnt by order of the Inquisition (1316).
The Council of Treves (1310), which condemns the
practices of sorcery, but confines itself to inflicting
on those guilty of it the pain of excommunication,
belongs to the same epoch. After Alexander IV,
sorcery, without being in itself a heresy, was sometimes complicated by heretical accessories. There
was still one step to go in order to assimilate sorcery
to heresy. It was taken by John XXII. In the Constitution *Super illius specula* (1326) this Pope proclaims with grief the great number of Christians

> ' who ally themselves with death and make a pact
> with hell, who sacrifice to the demons, make or
> have made images, rings, mirrors, phials or other
> analogous objects, intended to serve as bonds to
> hold the demons, who ask questions of the demons,
> obtain answers to them and have recourse to the
> demons to satisfy their depraved desires.'

In conclusion, all these pacts with the demon have
attached to them the same penalties as heresy.

Now let us see how this legislation works.

Ever since the last years of the twelfth century the bishops had been charged by the Papacy with the task of seeking out heretics and bringing them to their tribunals to chastise them. But they brought no zeal to their mission. Seeing their negligence, Pope Gregory IX, he, in fact, who introduced into the Canon Law the torment of fire, took from them the duty which they carried out so ill, and confided the task of seeking out heretics to the Dominicans and Franciscans. In other words, he founded the Inquisition.

When sorcery was assimilated to heresy, it came under the Inquisition. Pope John XXII extended the powers of the Inquisitors who, until then, had only hunted heretics, and he charged them to seek out sorcerers. Never was mission better fulfilled. The inquisitors showed themselves worthy of the confidence which the Papacy put in them, and they ferreted out sorcerers everywhere. Two of them have left a fadeless memory in the history of sorcery. They are the Dominicans Institoris and Sprenger. Sent by Innocent VIII into High Germany (Bavaria and the country round) they gave to their master a report which traced out a frightful picture of the state of souls. Innocent VIII who, before becoming Pope, had procreated more than a dozen bastards, was not scrupulous in matters of morality. But he upheld with ferocious zeal the purity of the faith. Terrified by the information which came to him from Germany, he thought it necessary to publish it, in order to put the whole of Christendom on its guard against the peril that menaced it. This is one of the objects of the famous Bull *Summis Desiderantes* (5th December 1584), in which we read :

'It has indeed lately come to Our ears, not without afflicting Us with bitter sorrow, that in some parts of Northern Germany, as well as in the provinces, townships, territories, districts and dioceses of Mainz, Cologne, Treves, Salzburg and Bremen, many people of both sexes, unmindful of their own salvation and straying from the Catholic Faith, have abandoned themselves to conjurations and other accursed charms and crafts, enormities and horrid offences, have slain infants yet in the mother's womb, as also the offspring of cattle, have blasted the produce of the earth, the grapes of the vine, the fruits of the trees, nay, men and women, beasts of burthen, herd-beasts, as well as animals of other kinds, vineyards, orchards, meadows, pasture-land, corn, wheat, and all other cereals ; these wretches, furthermore, afflict and torment men and women, beasts of burthen, herd-beasts, as well as animals of other kinds with terrible and piteous pains and sore diseases, both internal and external ; they hinder men from performing the sexual act and women from conceiving, whence husbands cannot know their wives, nor wives receive their husbands. . . .'

Having denounced the evil, the Pope shows the means to cure it. In reality, the remedy was in the hands of the inquisitors Institoris and Sprenger. But these men of God received a check from the clergy of

The Devils Astaroth, Abaddon and Mammon   Tibutus, Asmodeus and the Incubus

Germany, who set obstacles in their path and prevented them from acting. The Pope insists, under pain of the gravest penalty, that this opposition shall cease. Henceforth his representatives shall exercise in complete liberty their mission of salvation; the recalcitrants shall, at need, be delivered up to the secular arm.

To the apostolate of action Institoris and Sprenger added the apostolate of the pen. After they had, during several years, repressed witchcraft in High Germany, they published the celebrated *Malleus Maleficarum*, which for long was the code of the inquisitors.

I shall not overstep my rôle of reporter by noting here the observations which Innocent VIII's Bull has suggested to two Catholic writers of our own time. One of them, Pastor, says in his *Histoire des papes*, 5, 339:

'The pope, personally, might have been convinced of the reality of the facts; this has no importance. His opinion in this matter has only the value of a pontifical decision upon a question outside dogma, for example, a dispute as to the possession of a benefice.'

The other, the abbé Vacandard, replies to Pastor (*L'Inquisition*, p. 241):

'The learned historian here lets himself go. The conviction of the pope "imports" a great deal in this matter. A number of canonists have availed themselves of it to propagate the same

R

doctrine, as did the inquisitors, who drew from it practical consequences.'

In conclusion, let us note that, in several countries the Papacy was dispossessed by the civil power of its right of action against the sorcerers. In France, this happened about the end of the fourteenth century (1390). At that date the parliament[1] of Paris reserved to itself the right of judging sorcerers. In Germany the civil power arrogated to itself the same right at the beginning of the sixteenth century. Thus, in France and in Germany the sorcerers escaped from the Papacy, which had taken the initiative in pursuing them, and came under the civil tribunals. However, they gained nothing by the change.

[1] The French *parlement* was a body of mixed judicial and other functions. By 1789 twelve *parlements* had developed in the provinces from the original court (itself a subdivision of the Conseil du Roi) at Paris.—*Translator.*

Chapter XXXIII

RESULTS OF THE LEGISLATION AGAINST SORCERERS

First I will submit to the reader a few particular cases. They will prepare the way for a general survey which will follow them.

§ 1. THE SORCERERS OF ARRAS

This affair began at Langres, in 1459, by the condemnation of the magician Robinet de Vaulx who, before going to the stake, declared that he had met in the Witches' Sabbath a woman of evil life called Deniselle. Deniselle, a native of Douai, came under the tribunal of Arras. Put to the torture by the inquisitors of this town, she confessed that she had gone to the Sabbath and there had met Jean la Vitte. He, tortured in his turn, named divers persons who had gone with him to the Sabbath. Six arrests were instantly carried out. This occurred twenty-four years before the Bull of Innocent VIII. At this period the law was established, but its application was relatively rare. Some of the judges, who would have burnt one sorcerer without compunction, hesitated to act against several victims with all the rigour of the law. But others, more zealous, explained that the salvation of Christendom was involved, that there were sorcerers everywhere, even among the bishops and cardinals, that it was necessary to take energetic measures against the evil, and that a mistaken pity would be disastrous, not only for religion but for the very bases of social order. They carried their point. On the 10th May 1360 all the accused, including Deniselle and Jean la Vitte, were brought out to a scaffold erected in front of the palace of the bishop of Arras. Each had upon his head a mitre decorated with pictures which represented him adoring the Devil. It is unnecessary to say that a considerable crowd witnessed the ceremony. The inquisitor spoke and described what passed at the Sabbath; then, turning towards the accused, he asked them whether they had gone to the Sabbath, where the sorcerers gathered. They replied in the affirmative. Then fire was set to the scaffold. Immediately the unhappy wretches uttered frightful cries, declaring that they were innocent, and that their avowals, extorted at one time by the torture and at another by the promise of pardon, were valueless. But the flames soon reduced them to silence. Meanwhile, other sorcerers had been denounced and arrested. On the 7th July five of them were burnt. On the 22nd October four others appeared before the judges. One of them, Pierre de Carieulx, had very frequently gone to the Sabbath. He had kissed the Devil, who was transformed into a monkey, under his tail. He had given up his soul to Satan by a pact signed in his blood. He had handed to another sorcerer the consecrated Host which, mingled with the powdered bones of hanged men and with the blood of young children, had been used to prepare an infernal powder. But, when he was invited to confirm these avowals, he refused, declaring that they had been torn from him by torture. Given up to the secular arm, he went to the stake that very day.

Another, the Chevalier de Beauffort, had gone to the Sabbath three times, twice on foot and another time flying through the air on a stick anointed with a magic unguent. He had refused to give his soul to Satan, but he had given him four of his hairs. Beauffort admitted that the facts of which he was accused were true, and he implored the pity of the judges. As a reward for these avowals, which he had made without torture and which he had not retracted, the culprit was exempted from the stake. The inquisitor contented himself with scourging him and inflicting on him seven years' imprisonment and a total fine of fifteen thousand livres, out of which fifteen hundred were to go to the Inquisition and four thousand to the Duke of Burgundy.

A third, Jean Tacquet, an échevin of Arras, admitted that he had gone to the Sabbath ten times at least. He had tried to throw off the yoke of the Devil, who had constrained him to obedience by striking him blows with the sinews of an ox. He was sentenced to the scourge, ten years of imprisonment and a fine of fourteen hundred livres, of which two hundred were for the Inquisition.

A fourth, Huguet Aubry, in spite of the cruel torture to which he was subjected, had made no avowal. Nine witnesses accused him. He was promised that he would be treated with indulgence if he consented to admit his crimes. He refused, and confined himself to imploring, upon his knees, the pity of the judges. He was condemned to twenty years' imprisonment on bread and water.

Others accused were set free upon payment of fines. It was against the law. And, besides, the law had already been violated by the condemnation to twenty years' imprisonment of Huguet Aubry who, accused by nine witnesses, should normally have gone to the stake. The procedure against the sorcerers of Arras, which had begun well, went awry in the end. This *dénouement* was attributed to the Lords of Croy who, feeling that they themselves were threatened, intervened with the Duke of Burgundy. The latter ought, legally, to have been condemned for putting obstacles in the way of ecclesiastical jurisdiction, but Rome left him alone.

§ 2.   THE BASQUE SORCERERS

In 1609 the sorcerers ravaged twenty-seven parishes in the Bayonne country. Henry IV, being informed of the evil, charged the magistrates of Bordeaux with its suppression. One of them, the Councillor Delancre, consigned his witness to a book, in which we read (*Tableau de l'inconstance des mauvais anges*, p. 13):

' They have found a way to ravish women from the arms of their husbands and, doing forced violence to this sacred tie of marriage, they have committed adultery and enjoyed them in the presence of their husbands, who, like statues and motionless and dishonoured onlookers, saw their honour ravished without being able to stop it ; the woman dumb, wrapped in a forced silence ; and the husband, himself without help, constrained to suffer his shame with open eyes and folded arms.'

Then he enumerates the practices of the sorcerers in the following précis :

' To dance indecently, to revel periodically, to couple diabolically, to blaspheme scandalously, to avenge themselves insidiously, to run after every horrible, filthy and unnatural desire brutally, to hold toads and vipers, lizards and every kind of poison preciously, to love a smelling goat ardently, to caress it amorously.'

The magistrates set to work with a will. They began by arresting the most suspect individuals. When they were put to the torture, the sorcerers heard Beelzebub, who cried out to them that they should stand fast, and he promised soon to come himself to burn their executioners. Upon the rack their pains threw them into ecstasy and, when they were withdrawn from it, they declared that they had tasted ineffable joys.

They named their accomplices, and these, in their turn, were also arrested. Women, held to be witches, went to the stake. Delancre says of one of them :

' The Almighty, in order to make manifest the abomination and to show that she was truly a witch, permitted that from above her head there came forth a swarm of toads, upon which the people rushed at her so fiercely with sticks and stones that she was more stoned than burnt. But in spite of all the assault it was beyond the power of the people to put to death a black toad, which triumphed over the flames, the sticks and the stones . . . and escaped, as an immortal demon, to such a place that no one was ever able to find it.'

Several priests were sent before the tribunal. One of them, of advanced age, did not seem in possession of his faculties, and his relatives confirmed that he had lost his reason. But two witnesses affirmed that they had seen him at the Sabbath. He himself, moreover, admitted that he had been there, and that he had renounced his priesthood to give himself to the Devil. The wretched old man was degraded by the bishop of Dax, then conducted into the parish confided to his administrator, there to be burnt. Delancre says of this :

'The death of this priest made a great impression in the town of Bayonne. . . . Terror spread throughout the whole country, to such an extent that the inhabitants took liberty and assurance to denounce other clergy. . . . So many innocent children and other witnesses, strangers to the parish, disinterested, and of every kind, told us ingenuously that they had seen certain priests at the sabbath, that we were constrained, seeing that it was they who spoilt and infested the country, to take some of the most heavily accused. We took first seven of them, among the most notable persons in the whole country. . . .'

Two of these priests were burnt. The bishop of Dax managed to save the other five. Finally, the magistrates, who had powers only for a limited period, returned to Bordeaux. They had succeeded in burning about eighty sorcerers. But many others, who had crossed the border, fell into the power of the Spanish Inquisition and they, too, were burnt.

§ 3.   THE PRIEST GAUFRIDI

We have seen above that this priest was accused of the crime of sorcery by two Ursulines of the convent of Aix. When he was brought before the Dominican Michaelis, Gaufridi defended himself vigorously. But the denunciations made by the demoniacs in the course of the exorcisms, were reputed to be infallible. And, besides, the two nuns, Madeleine and Louise, who were present at the interrogatory, overwhelmed the accused with curses. Here is one of Louise's speeches :

> ' Louis Gaufridi, outside, makes believe that he is a saint ; however, inside he is full of iniquity. He feigns to abstain from flesh ; nevertheless, he makes himself drunk with the flesh of little children. . . . O Michaelis, the little children whom he has eaten, the others whom he has suffocated and afterwards dug up, all cry before God for vengeance upon crimes so execrable.'

And Madeleine explained as follows Gaufridi's distaste for food :

'Much he cares for your salt fish or your eggs! He eats good smoking flesh of little children, which is brought to him invisibly from the synagogue.'

These so precise and peremptory accusations fortified the conviction of the inquisitor, Michaelis, who threw Gaufridi into prison. In the grip of unhappiness and isolation, the wretched priest let himself be cast down. The ill from which he suffered was further aggravated by two monks, who were given the mission of converting him, and did not cease to harass him. His imagination became exalted and his reason ended by giving way. He admitted that he had made a pact with Lucifer, and that he had received from this infernal being the power of attaching to himself every woman whom he could reach with his breath. This is what we read in the *Confessions made by Messire Louis Gaufridi:*

'More than a thousand persons have been poisoned by the irresistible attraction of my breath, which filled them with passion. The lady of La Palude, the mother of Madeleine, was fascinated like so many others. But Madeleine was taken with an unreasoning love, and abandoned herself to me, both in the sabbath and outside the sabbath. . . . I was marked at the sabbath of my consentment and I had Madeleine marked on her head, on her heart, on her belly, on her thighs, on her legs, on her feet. . . .'

These *Confessions* seemed a superabundant proof of the crime of sorcery. On the 30th April 1611, the priest, Louis Gaufridi, was publicly degraded at Aix. After which, head and feet bare, a rope around his neck, holding in his hand a burning torch, the wretched man was led through the town by the executioner. When he had come before the porch of the cathedral, he asked pardon of God, of the Church and of the king. Then he went to the square, where the pyre was entirely ready. He mounted it, was devoured by the flames, and his ashes were thrown to the winds.

§ 4. URBAIN GRANDIER

Among the victims of the trials for sorcery, one of the most famous was, without contradiction, Urbain Grandier, the curé of Saint Pierre of Loudun, of whom we have already heard. As we know, the possessed Ursulines replied to the questions of the exorcist that the author of the lamentable state in which they were was Grandier. This answer, which emanated from the Devil, who held them in his possession was, according to the legislation of the Ritual, decisive; Grandier, in spite of his denials, was thrown into prison and his trial had for its object the obtaining of proofs confirmatory of the allegations of Satan. The proofs obtained numbered three.

The first was constituted by the marks of the Devil. Jeanne de Belcies, the superior, declared that Satan had left his mark on five places on Grandier's body, and that in these five places the sorcerer-priest would feel nothing. This allegation was submitted to verification. The prisoner, stripped naked, was shaved all over his body and then given up to a surgeon who, armed with a needle, sought out the insensitive places. All the stabs of the needle which rained upon the victim made him utter piercing shrieks. All except two, to which the patient remained insensitive. Thus Satan had marked two places with his claws on the body of the sorcerer. This result did not accord with the declaration of Jeanne de Belcies, who had denounced five marks. A sceptic might have thought that the surgeon had forgotten or misunderstood the instructions, which enjoined him to find five of these marks. But the king's counsellor charged with the direction of the trial concluded, on the contrary, that the result was satisfactory, and that Grandier had made a pact with the Devil.

The second proof was furnished by the confrontation of the sorcerer with his victims. Grandier was brought into the presence of the possessed nuns. They, upon seeing him, overwhelmed him with vociferation and cursing, and declared him the author of their ills, and threw their shoes at his face. Then, seized with violent convulsions, they made ready to strangle him. An end was put to this horrible séance by taking the accused back to his prison; for the second time, he was convicted of the crime.

The third proof was afforded by the following depositions of a special kind. A woman of Loudun, presenting herself before the judges, avowed that she had felt a violent love for Grandier following a look which the latter had fixed upon her when he was giving her communion. Another woman recognised that she had been a prey to the same passion following upon a handclasp given to the curé of Saint Pierre. A third had, she too, experienced guilty desires in the course of a procession in which her eyes had encountered those of the curé, who was officiating. Then came nuns who, having seen Grandier in their convent, night and day, had become infatuated with him. Finally a woman declared that she had had carnal relations with the said curé, who had even proposed to take her to the Witches' Sabbath. Manifestly, only a magician would be able to inspire women with such violent and such uncontrolled love.

After they had prayed and asked guidance from heaven for several weeks, the judges pronounced sentence on the 18th August 1634, by the terms of which Urbain Grandier, found guilty of sorcery, was condemned to the torment of fire, but not without first revealing the names of his accomplices.

Pronounced in the early morning, the sentence was to be executed on the same day. The evening was reserved for the pyre : the morning was consecrated to the reception of the condemned man's revelations. Brought before his judges for the last time, Grandier, whose hands were tied behind his back, said :

'I call God the Father, the Son and the Holy Ghost, and the Virgin, my unique advocates, to witness that I have never been a magician, that I have never committed sacrilege . . . that I have no other belief than that of our mother, the Holy Catholic, Apostolic and Roman Church. ...'

This protestation of innocence removed all question of complicity. Nevertheless, the judges interrogated the condemned man on this point ; he replied with energy : ' I have no accomplices.' Then, conformable to the law, recourse was had to torture to constrain the culprit to the avowals which he had refused to make spontaneously. Each of Grandier's legs was enclosed between two planks. Then the two planks were fastened together with two stout ropes and, with a mallet, wedges were forced between the planks in the middle. The monks themselves carried out this task. Under the stab of the pain the patient made the avowal that was insisted on, and declared himself guilty of magic. But this weakness lasted only a moment. Immediately, Grandier pronounced these words of retraction :

' O my soul! What have I said ? Hast thou murmured against God and against thy Creator ? Nay, messires, I am not a magician and I never was one. My God, my Father, my sweet Jesus, saviour and redeemer, do not abandon me. May neither the flames nor the torture have any force to make me deny Him who has given me life.'

It was the middle of the day. The executioners withdrew to take their meal and the victim awaited the final torture, which was fixed for five o'clock. Then Grandier, whose legs were half broken, was hoisted on to a cart and taken to the Saint-Croix square, where an enormous crowd had gathered. He was sat on a seat fixed to a stake upon the pyre. The monks struck him on the face with the crucifix under the pretext of giving it him to kiss, and as the sufferer turned his head aside to avoid the blows, they cried out indignantly : ' You see him! He is repulsing the image of the Lord, the Saviour!' Those who were condemned bore around their necks a rope, with which ordinarily they were strangled before being given to the fire ; and Grandier had been promised that this measure of mercy would be applied to him. But, at the last moment, the exorcists made several knots in the rope, so that the executioner could not tighten it. A monk set fire to the pyre, and Grandier was burnt alive at the moment when he was uttering these words from the *Psalms:*

' O Lord! have mercy upon me according to thy loving-kindness.'

§ 5. A GENERAL SURVEY

Tertullian tells us that the blood of the martyrs was a sowing of seed for Christians, and that many pagans were attracted to Christianity by the hatred of which it was the object. The legislation of the Church against sorcery had the same result. Never had there been so many sorcerers as on the day when the Papacy raged against them. But the more ferocious the measures employed against them, the more their number increased. Boguet gives us some precious information on this point. He was chief

judge at Saint-Claude about 1600. He condemned
many sorcerers. This is what he says at the beginning
of his *Discours des sorciers avec son avis en fait de
sorcellerie:*

'I hold that sorcerers could raise an army equal
to that of Xerxes which, nevertheless, was of
eighteen hundred thousand men. . . . For if . . .
under Charles IX, there were in France alone three
hundred thousand, how great are we to estimate
the number that could be met with in other lands
and countries of the world ? And do we not
believe, too, that since this time they have increased by half ? For my part, I have not the
slightest doubt of it. All the more as, if we look
only at our neighbours, we see them absolutely
swarming with the same wretched and damnable
vermin. Germany is scarcely busied with anything
else than making fires for them. Switzerland, on
this account, is depeopling many of its villages.
Lorraine shows to the traveller thousands and
thousands of stakes whereto sorcerers are chained.
And for us (for we are no more exempt than the
others) we see the ordinary executions, which are
being carried out in several districts. Savoy—for
it sends us every day an infinity of people who are
possessed with demons who, when they are cast
out, say that they have been put into the bodies of
these wretches by sorcerers—asserts that the chief
of those whom we have had burnt here, in Burgundy, originally came forth thence. But what
judgement are we to give to France ? It is indeed

THE SABBATH, OR THE REUNION OF THE SORCERERS
An old sorcerer offers a child to Satan, who is
pictured as a he-goat
From a painting by Goya in the Prado

difficult to believe that she is purged of them. . . .
I do not speak of other more distant regions. No,
no, the sorcerers go everywhere by thousands,
they multiply in the earth like caterpillars in our
gardens. . . . I desire that they shall know that, if
results corresponded to my will, the earth would
soon be purged, for I would like them all to be put
into a single body, so that they might all be burnt
at the same time in one fire.'

Boguet says that Germany is, so to speak, occupied
in burning sorcerers. He is right. It was above all
in Germany that the sorcerers, tracked down by
Sprenger and Institoris, went to the stake ; it was
there, above all, that they swarmed. From this point
of view, the following letter of Father Canisius (now
canonised by Rome) is a document of the first importance, which it is necessary to know. This is what
this great apostle of the Roman Church writes (20th
November 1563) to the general of the Jesuits,
Lainez : [1]

' The witches, who multiply extraordinarily, are
being chastised. Their crimes are frightful. They
envy the fate of children, who have preserved the
grace of baptism, and wish to ravish it from them.
A great number of them make the little children
perish, and even devour their flesh, as they have
themselves avowed. Never were so many men
seen to give themselves to the Devil and make
alliance with him in Germany. The shamelessness
and cruelty of these perverse women, acting under

[1] Janssen, 8, 683.

S

the suggestions of Satan, reaches a scarcely credible degree. The authorities have published the avowals they have made in their prisons. In many towns these execrable vixens are burnt, enemies of human nature and of the Christian name. How many people are victims of their spells! They raise up tempests, they are the cause of the frightful catastrophes which desolate our fields. The most just Lord permits it, to punish the iniquities of the Christian people, who refuse to do penance.'

Finally, I would set before the reader the conclusions of Lea :

' Protestants and Catholics rivalled one another in murderous rage. Witches were no longer burnt separately or in couples, but by twenties and hundreds. A bishop of Geneva burnt, they said, five hundred in three months ; a bishop of Bamberg six hundred ; a bishop of Wurtzburg nine hundred. Eight hundred were condemned, probably at a single session, by the senate of Savoy. The intervention of Satan, by the intermediary of his worshippers, was so much an integral part of the convictions of the time, that every unusual phenomenon of Nature was attributed without hesitation to these infernal agents. The summer of 1586 was late in the Rhine provinces and the cold continued until June. That could only be a result of witchcraft, and the archbishop of Treves burnt a hundred and eighteen women and two men, from whom the avowal had been extorted that the prolongation of the winter was the work of their incantations. He was right to act promptly for, while they were going to the place of execution, the culprits declared that, if they had had three days more, they would have provoked a cold so intense that no verdure could have survived, and that all the fields and vineyards would have been stricken with sterility. Clearly the Inquisition had worthy disciples; but itself did not relax its efforts. Paramo states with pride that . . . in 1404, the Holy Office had burnt more than thirty thousand witches who, if they had enjoyed impunity, would have brought the whole world to utter ruin.'

CHAPTER XXXIV

THE ABROGATION OF THE LAWS AGAINST SORCERERS

WE have seen that, from the end of the fourteenth century, the parliament of Paris reserved to itself the right of judging sorcerers. Venice, at the end of the sixteenth century, followed this example. After having allowed the pontifical inquisitors to burn witches and sorcerers at their pleasure, she at last protested (1520). Surprised by so much insolence, Pope Leo X fulminated, in 1521, the Bull *Honestis*, in which he enjoined upon the Council of Venice, under the gravest penalties, that they should carry out sentences given by the Church against witches. But the Council, refusing to let itself be frightened by the pontifical threats, itself fixed its statute of sorcerers.

However, we should be in error if we attributed great importance to these incidents. When the sorcerers of France passed from ecclesiastical to civil jurisdiction, they gained nothing by the change, and continued to be burnt as in the past. As for the government of Venice, it maintained the general lines of the trial of witches and confined itself to certain liberal modifications. In short, the acts of independence accomplished at Paris in 1390 and at

Venice in 1521 humiliated the Papacy; they did not go further. And they could not go further because, during the whole of the fifteenth century, and even longer, the sorcerers, considered as the tools of the Devil, were made responsible for public calamities. No torment seemed too cruel to chastise their crimes. Such was the desire of the mentality of the epoch. This mentality had to disappear or, at least, to diminish and weaken before a change in the legislation against sorcerers was possible. As long as it reigned, the sorcerers continued to be burnt, as well by the civil authorities as by the Church, among the Protestants as among the Catholics. We must find out at what date public opinion began to turn, at least in the higher spheres. But first of all, let us speak of him who was the first workman in bringing about this salutary change.

§ 1. JEAN WIER: HIS SYSTEM AND HIS METHOD

Jean Wier (or Weyer), who was born in Brabant in 1515, and who died in Westphalia in 1588, was, during the last thirty years of his life, chief physician to the Duke of Cleves. He studied the diabolic phenomena, and he consigned the results of his researches to numerous writings. His principal book is a great work in six parts, entitled *De præstigiis dæmonum et incantationibus ac veneficiis*. This work, published at Bale in 1564, was translated into French for the first time by Grevin in 1567, a second time by Simon

Goulart in 1579. This second translation was re-printed in 1885. It is entitled *Histoires, disputes et discours des illusions et impostures du diable, etc.*

Jean Wier believed in demons and in demoniac possession. Here are a few samples of the cases which he sought out (the references are to the French edition of 1885):

'4, 8: In the year 1566, on the 18th March, in the town of Amsterdam in Holland, there occurred a memorable case set down in writing by Messire Adrian Nicolai, chancellor of Guelders, as follows:

' Two months or so ago, he says, thirty children in this town began to be tormented in a strange manner as if they were maniacs or mad. At intervals, they threw themselves on the ground, and this torment lasted for half an hour or an hour at most. Having got up again, they remembered nothing of their ill, nor of what they had done, but they thought that they had slept. The doctors of whom advice was asked achieved nothing, because they saw in this a natural disease. Then the parents, suspecting that the sorcerers were concerned, had recourse to them. But they, with all their sorceries, could do nothing. Finally it was thought that these children were possessed, and recourse was had to several exorcists, particularly because the children said, without thinking, many things which were beyond their range and their age. These exorcists, according to their custom, began by readings and conjurations, and brought to bear all their resources against the devils. But they wasted their time. While they were carrying out their exorcisms, the children vomited needles, pins, thimbles . . . hairs, and other suchlike things. For all that, the children were not cured, but they fell again into the same ill from time to time, to the great astonishment of everyone, because of the novelty of such a strange spectacle.

'I say, as my opinion on this matter, that God permitted the Devil to dazzle the eyes of the on-lookers by throwing such substances out of the mouths of the children because their parents had not had recourse to legitimate means; that these things had never entered into their bodies, and that the Devil had not been able to introduce them through the throat, which is too narrow. Now he played this horrible drama in this place renowned above all others, not only to advance and augment the fame which he had for sorcery and enchant-ment, but also in order to charge with that crime several innocent women, and subsequently have them burnt alive as guilty in this matter. . . . This is how this crafty fellow thought to profit by his efforts. And God often permits that people shall be thus afflicted to try the firmness of our faith. However, he strictly forbade the Devil to do any harm to the children.

'4, 10 : The torments which the devils inflicted upon certain nuns at Uvertet, in the country of Horn, are wondrous and horrible. It is related that the beginning came with a poor woman who, in Lent, borrowed from the nuns three pounds of salt, and afterwards gave back twice as much at Easter. From that moment they began to find in their dormitory little white bullets, like comfits made of sugar, which were salt to the taste. . . . A little while after, they perceived something which seemed to complain like a sick man. But sometimes they heard a voice, which admonished certain nuns that they should rise and come to the help of their suffering sister ; but when these had risen to go to her, they found nothing. . . . Sometimes they were drawn from their beds by the feet and dragged a considerable distance and tickled under the sole to such an extent that they feared they would die of laughing. . . . Some were raised into the air to the height of a man's head, then were instantly thrown to earth. . . . It happened that two nuns among the sick ones . . . began to speak of a black cat which, they said, was in their dormitory and had been shut in a basket by a dame whom they named and who lived in the town. These things, being heard by another nun who was not ill, she related it to the Mother Superior who, accompanied by two or three nuns, went to find the basket ; it was opened, and there came forth from it a cat, which fled. . . . Because of this, the poor woman was suspected of being a witch, and was put into prison with seven others, who were brought there afterwards. Among others, there was a matron, the oldest of them all, who, by the testimony of neighbours and of the poor, was so charitable towards the suffering, that she herself had endured want because of it. . . . Now there can be no doubt that Satan did possess these nuns. He, thinking to have convenient occasion to deceive by the means of this salt, which the poor woman had given back, took pains to make these credulous nuns believe that it was a matter of sorcery, in order to wound the good name of this innocent matron. . . . Further, God permitted the Devil to torment them, either in order that these nuns might be tried or chastised or else because of their incredulity. Now they were found to lack firm and stable faith, since they traced the cause of these ills to a woman and not to the will of God. And, from that follows the Satanic counsel of the two nuns, which was invented by the Devil, who was the conductor of their lying words, in order to imprint a perpetual mark upon the poor innocent woman whom they accused of sorcery. . . . Even if the cat was a natural one, we must not doubt that the Devil had put it into the basket. And, indeed, I think rather that it was the Devil himself, in the form of a cat. And so we see that, in all this drama, God limited his power to such an extent that she whom he lifted up and let fall got no harm of it, even when it seemed that she was dead.

'4, 12: The nuns of the convent of Nazareth at Cologne were tormented almost in the manner described above, for, having been for several years afflicted, worried and diversely and in several ways stormed at by the Devil, they were yet more prodigiously and horribly treated. In the year 1564, when . . . they were thrown to the ground, their

bellies on high and thrown back as if to have commerce with man ; during which act they kept their
eyes shut, which they afterwards opened in great
shame and as if they had endured great pain. A
young girl named Gertrude, aged fourteen, who
had been shut up in this nunnery, gave the first
occasion to this trouble. She had often experienced
the mad apparitions in her bed. . . . A companion
had lain down on a couch expressly to defend her
against this apparition. This poor child took fright
when she heard the noise of the struggle. Finally,
she became the resorting-place of the Devil ; she
was miserably afflicted with several contractions of
the nerves. . . . The same happened to several
others. And thus this plague, little by little, increased, all the more when these poor wretches
had recourse to illegitimate remedies.'

What are we to understand by ' illegitimate
remedies ? ' The text does not tell us. But elsewhere
we learn that this formula means Catholic exorcisms.
One chapter of the book (5, 23) is entitled :

' The serious and abominable abuse of the
exorcist priests.'

In it we read the following :

' There are certain men, foolish, rash and
audacious, who call themselves Churchpeople, but
who are more than worldly by their villainous and
filthy life . . . who, being called in to cure those
who are thought to be possessed or bewitched, by
their accustomed exorcisms and by their accomplishment of certain ceremonies, hasten to cure the

possessed or to cast out the Devil. . . . These exorcists deserve to be put among the enchanters and sorcerers. . . . The bewitched person holds a candle in his hand and kneels on the ground. . . . Holy water is thrown over him and a stole is attached round his neck and, besides oraisons, popular litanies are recited. . . . Then they use exorcisms, which are continued at least three times a week, in order that, by multiplying the intercessions, the grace of health shall be obtained. The theologians, who were the authors of the *Malleus Maleficarum*, prescribe this form of exorcism against the evident wish of Christ, who said . . . " When ye pray, use not vain repetitions, as the Gentiles do : for they think that they shall be heard for their much speaking. Be not therefore like unto them : for your Father knoweth what things ye have need of, before ye ask him." '

This language ceases to surprise us, when we learn that Wier is a Protestant. The rites in use in the Roman Church are, in his eyes, contemptible stupidities, and he does not conceal the horror with which he is inspired by the filthy lives of the exorcist monks. Convinced that the demons do sometimes establish themselves in the bodies of certain persons, he does not condemn the efforts which seek to expel them. But on condition that the procedure recommended by Scripture is employed. One of these means is prayer, whose efficacity is witnessed by the example of the prophet Elijah and by the apostle James. Another method is fasting, to which alms-giving should be added. Wier prescribes recourse to these three exorcisms (5, 31-33). He seems to attach particular importance to fasting. He says (31):

'And so also, fasting must be ordered if, peradventure, the flesh, in order to be more at its ease, has entered into arrogance, and by this means has given place to the Devil: in order that, being held in by this bridle-rein, it shall be returned to its right place. Thus Porphyry writes that fasting and chastity are greatly to be praised; not that by these two God is principally appeased, but in order that the Devils who take pleasure in blood and in villainy and who, in order to enjoy it, enter into the bodies of those who use them, shall be prevented and driven behind us.'

However, neither prayer, nor alms, nor fasting itself are infallibly efficacious. The supreme resource of the victims of the Devil is patience and submission to the will of God, without which nothing can come to pass. Listen to Jean Wier (5, 29):

'The afflicted must be diligently excited to an invincible patience against the assaults of the Devil and a constant confidence in God by the example of our ancient Fathers, as by the example of Saint Antony of Egypt. . . . Saint Antony, being healed, understood truly that Jesus healed him, and he said to him: "Where were you, good Jesus, where were you? Why did you not help me in the beginning, to heal my sores?" A voice answered him: "Antony, I was present here, but I waited, because of your combat, which it pleased me to contemplate first. And henceforth your name shall be renowned by all the world, because you have shown yourself a valiant warrior." '

In short, nothing comes to pass save by the will of God, and God likes to see the Christian at grips with the Devil. But then, to pray, to give alms and to fast to obtain the expulsion of Satan, is not that working against the will of God?

Jean Wier, who believes in the reality of possession, does not believe in licentious demons nor in the maleficence of sorcerers. The latter are, according to him, deceived by the Devil, who leads their imagination astray. Jean Wier, then, rejects witchcraft: it is because of that that his book marks an epoch in the history of the emancipation of the human spirit.

§ 2. THE EVOLUTION OF PUBLIC OPINION

Jean Wier came into direct opposition to general public opinion. He very soon experienced its hostility. His book was put on the Index, and many refutations were written against it. Remigius, a magistrate of Lorraine, published a book, in which Jean Wier was declared to be :[1]

'Ignorant in matters of law, revolting in his theories and worthy of the most rigorous chastisements.'

And this book bore a singularly eloquent title: *Dæmonolatria, a treatise upon sorcery by the noble,*

[1] Janssen, 8, 632 *seq.*

most honourable and most learned doctor Nicholas Remigius, containing wondrous histories of witches burnt alive in the duchy of Lorraine, to the number of more than eight hundred, a book most useful and pleasant to read.

The curé Agricola showed that society would perish if witches were not proceeded against with all vigour, and he refuted the objections intended to make mercy prevail. One of these objections based itself upon the fact that the great number of witches would make it difficult to attempt their extermination. Agricola answers :

' When authority chastises the malefactors and stirrers up of trouble in gross, it counts the expense as nothing. It is the same when it undertakes a war, often upon slight pretexts. Much the more should it find nothing too onerous when it is a question of executing the orders of God. . . . It has the duty of chastising this diabolic breed, for the edification, consolation and salvation of the whole Christian people. . . . And authority can all the less allege reasons of economy when it abstains from having witches executed, because it has in its own hands the means of recouping itself by confiscating the goods of the tortured, as is indeed practised in more than one territory of the Empire, and the thing is most just and equitable. It must also be remembered that when the goods or inheritances of the rich accomplices of the sorcerers are confiscated, all the harm that they have cost to men, to beasts and to the harvests, is thereby repaired.'

However, in spite of the clamorous attacks to which he was subjected, Jean Wier slowly but steadily enlightened people's minds. A few theologians—a very few—notably the Jesuits Laymann, Tanner and Spee,[1] opened their eyes, in different degrees, to the truth and perceived, or at least, glimpsed, the fact that the sorcerers were mentally disordered rather than criminal persons.

Psychological evolution, which the theologians themselves did not escape, also took place in certain cultivated laymen. Proof of this came in 1660, the date at which the parliament of Paris ceased to believe in sorcerers.

Several parliaments followed the example of Paris. However, the traditional spirit was not completely banished from French justice. The parliament of Rouen, notably, persisted in maintaining the good old customs. In 1670 it had arrested, at one stroke, thirty-four sorcerers. But the Royal Council intervened. By a first measure it commuted the sentence of death that had been delivered against four of these wretched people into mere banishment, and it prescribed that the other executions must be abandoned. Then, two years later (1672), it closed all the proceedings instituted in Normandy in the matter of witchcraft, and it recommended that the prison doors should be opened to release all prisoners held solely for this crime.[2] Then the councillors of the parlia-

---

[1] Janssen, 8, 682.

[2] Floquet, *Histoire du parlement de Normandie*, 5, 718; Garinet, *Histoire de la magie en France*, p. 337.

ment of Rouen sent to the king a respectful *request*, in which they said :

  ' Sire . . . there having come a declaration from Your Majesty, commuting the pain of death given in judgement against the condemned into perpetual banishment from the province . . . your parliament has thought best, Sire, in order to satisfy the intentions of Your Majesty, that, as it concerned one of the greatest crimes that can be committed, it ought to make known to you the general and uniform sentiment of the whole company, since there is at stake the glory of God and the relief of your peoples, who groan under the fear of the threats of this kind of person, *of whom they daily feel the effects by mortal and extraordinary maladies and by the surprising losses of their goods.*

  ' Sire, Your Majesty is well aware that there is no kind of crime so opposed to God as that of sorcery, which destroys the foundations of religion and draws after itself strange abominations. It is for this reason, Sire, that Scripture pronounces the pain of death against those who commit it, and the Church and the holy Fathers have hurled anathema to try to abolish it. . . . Your parliaments, in their decrees, adjust the penalties to the proofs at the trials which they judge, and that of your province of Normandy has not often found that its jurisprudence has been different from that of any other, since all the books dealing with these matters relate an infinity of decrees which have been given for

THE DEVIL IN THE NINETEENTH CENTURY—IN
ROMANTIC COSTUME

the condemnation of sorcerers to the flames, and
to the wheel, and to other tortures.'

Here the councillors give a list of the chief decrees
pronounced against sorcerers by the different parliaments of France. They recall that the parliament of
Paris condemned many criminals who, according to
their own admissions, had taken part in the Sabbath,
and had there adored the Devil, disguised as a goat,
and had then given themselves to ' illicit couplings.'
They mention the proceedings of other parliaments ;
they recall, in particular, the condemnation by the
parliament of Toulouse, in 1557, of four hundred
accused. They conclude :

' And, because of all these considerations, Sire,
the officers of your parliament hope that Your
Majesty's justice will hold the very humble repre-
sentations which they take the liberty of making
as agreeable : and being obliged, for the acquit-
ment of their conscience and the duty of their
charges, to let you know that the decrees which
have been uttered in the judgement of the sorcerers
in their province have been given with ripe de-
liberation . . . and for the good of your subjects, of
whom none can be sure that they are protected
from their malevolence. May your justice suffer
the execution of the decrees in the form in which
they were given, and permit us to continue the
examination and judgement in the trials of the
persons accused of sorcery, and may the piety of
Your Majesty not suffer it that in your reign
opinions shall be introduced contrary to the prin-

T

ciples of the religion for which, Sire, Your Majesty
has always so gloriously used your devotion and
your arms.'

In the very year in which the councillors of the
parliament of Rouen wrote their moving plea, Malebranche published the *Recherche de la verité*, in which
there is an essay upon the contagious communication
of strong imaginations. In it we learn that 'men,
even the wisest, are led more by the imagination of
others than by the rules of reason.' And this assertion
is supported by the following considerations (2, 3, 6):

'Thus, in those places where sorcerers are
burnt, a great number of them is found because,
in those places where they are condemned to the
flames, it is truly believed that they are sorcerers,
and this belief is fortified by the discourse which
is held about them. Let their punishment cease
and let them be treated as madmen, and it will be
seen that, with the passage of time, there will no
longer be sorcerers, because those who were only
sorcerers in imagination, who are certainly the
greatest number, will return from their errors. . . .
It is thus in accordance with reason that several
parliaments do not punish sorcerers; in the districts in their provinces many fewer are found;
and the envy, the hatred and the malice of the
wicked cannot use this pretext to ruin the
innocent.'

Louis XIV had to choose between the request of
the parliament of Rouen and Malebranche's thesis.
He chose the latter. In 1682 a royal ordinance was

published, in which sorcerers are considered to be rogues or madmen, and in which it is prescribed that they shall be treated as such, the crime of sorcery being suppressed. In the course of the nineteenth century, this legislation was adopted by all the governments of the civilised world.[1] When, to-day, a judge sees a sorcerer brought to his tribunal, his only care is to find out if the accused is the victim of a disordered imagination or a rogue, who is exploiting the credulity of the ignorant. There are still, above all in the countryside, simple souls who believe in sorcerers, but legislators no longer believe in them.

[1] Hinschius, 5, 410.

CHAPTER XXXV

CONCLUSION

THE rival of God, whom he designed to equal;
seducer of the angels who, without him, would
have remained in the way of righteousness; slayer of
the Christ, whom he brought to crucifixion; the
irreconcilable enemy of the human race, which he
has overwhelmed with ills of every sort, the Devil
has a heavy record. To-day this career is ended, it
belongs to the past; Satan is a fallen prince. And his
fall is irrevocable, because it is caused by a definitive
elimination of his function.

Formerly mankind sought with anguish to know
why, under the government of a just God, unspeak-
able griefs tortured, every day, millions of men,
millions of children, millions of animals : and why,
too, every day, truth, virtue and innocence are
calumniated, scoffed at and trampled under foot :
why, in a word, the instinct of happiness and order
which we bear within us is brought up against the
universal and continual spectacle of suffering and
injustice.

That was a formidable problem to be solved; and
he who provided a solution was to be considered as
fulfilling the most elevated of all functions. One day
Satan offered himself to the Christians to solve the

problem, to fulfil the function. First he presented himself as a cruel creator of the world, at grips with a good, but invisible God. Then he donned a more modest livery, in which he was only an angel in revolt against a Creator filled with goodness. In each aspect he presented himself as the irreconcilable adversary of the good God, the implacable enemy of mankind. In each aspect he exerted himself to produce, by himself, all evil, to disengage the responsibility from God; in short, to resolve the enigma of evil.

The Christian world accepted the offer. Satan thus shouldered the responsibility of the suffering which torments human beings, of the injustices and crimes which stain humanity. For centuries he preserved this function, which he carried out to the general satisfaction.

But to-day this function is suppressed : it has no further reason for existence, and it is condemned to return into the void.

The function is suppressed : whence has the suppression come? From two opposite sides. Firstly, from those who withdraw the universe from the government of a personal God and would have the intervention in it of nothing save mechanical laws. It was necessary to put the divine holiness beyond all contact with evil. Once the personal God is suppressed, the problem is resolved radically, and there is no need at all to have recourse to the services of the Devil.

However, this solution has not, up to the present, gained more than a relatively small number of

adherents. The greater number of men, even to-day,
continue to believe : that is to say, to explain the
Universe by an intelligent and just God. And, for
these believers, evil is indeed a mysterious enigma.
But Satan is no longer called in, as of old, to resolve it. This attitude, which is most surprising, has
evidently a cause. Let us try to find it.

Man to-day has at his disposition two weapons
against evil : the spirit of solidarity, and science. The
spirit of solidarity which, even in the Middle Ages,
founded hospitals, has in our days suppressed slavery:
it is in process of suppressing war, and of diminishing
social inequalities. As for science, it has, with
Franklin, protected us from lightning ; with Pasteur,
for whom Jenner prepared the way, it has driven
from us many terrible diseases.

The spirit of solidarity and science, joining
together their efforts, have made Evil retreat. To
this first consequence another, of a psychological
order, has been added. It is this. Drunk with the
successes already obtained, man dreams of new con-
quests. He knows that social institutions, and science,
will not cease to pursue the enemy, to track it down.
He foresees their progress, in advance. And this
anticipated vision, at the same time as it enchants him,
captivates his attention. I have said that evil is, for
believers, a mysterious enigma. It must be added
that this enigma preoccupies them very little. They
think of it seldom indeed : their minds are turned
elsewhere. Happy to take part in the rout of the
enemy, they do not ask whence the enemy came. The
joy of victory conceals from them the problem of

origins. If they sought whence the evil proceeded, their eyes would turn immediately toward the rebel angel. But the explanation of evil does not preoccupy them. To take only one example, when the clergy are asked to bless a factory or a railway line, the preacher discourses of the admirable goodness of God, who has permitted man to tame and to domesticate the most formidable forces of Nature. But he takes good care not to explain why this so good God has delayed thus long in making this gift to man. The conquest, which puts an end to our destitution and assures our well-being, holds his attention: but the long centuries during which our ancestors, deprived of everything, groaned, leave him indifferent. It is this indifference that is fatal to Satan.

And I have still said nothing of the two supreme defeats which marked the dissolution of the infernal power. Formerly, Satan threw his power over certain persons whom he tortured, either by himself taking possession of their bodies, or by the intermediary of the sorcerers, who were his collaborators. Possession and Sorcery were like two provinces in which he reigned as a master, and in which his activity manifested itself to the human race by phenomena which were as violently striking as they were harmful. Now these two fiefs have been taken from him. Nowadays, possession is nothing but a neurosis, that is to say, a malady of the nervous system; its treatment depends upon medicine, and not upon the Church. As for the sorcerers' prowess, it is the product of hallucination unless—what is most frequently the case to-day—it does not proceed from fraud. And Satan, cast out from the refuge which, formerly, he found with the possessed and the sorcerers, and the witches, is like the Son of Man, of whom the Gospel tells us that He had nowhere to lay His head.

THE END

INDEX

CPSIA information can be obtained
at www.ICGtesting.com
Printed in the USA
BVOW09s1945060317
477786BV00008BA/144/P